INDIAN PRAIRIE PUBLIC LIBRARY DISTRICT

31946 00385 9813

D1274469

JAN 1 1 2007

2-10 2010 (5)
5/12 (7)
6-29-15 (13)

Indian Prairie Public Library District
401 Plainfield Road ~ Darien, IL 60561

CANDY
THE SWEET HISTORY

B E T H   K I M M E R L E

COLLECTORS PRESS

PORTLAND, OREGON

INDIAN PRAIRIE PUBLIC LIBRARY
401 Plainfield Road
Darien, IL 60561

Copyright © 2003 Collectors Press, Inc.

All rights reserved. No part of this book may be reproduced or transmitted in any form by any means, electronic or mechanical, including photocopying, recording, or by any information storage and retrieval system, without written permission of the publisher except where permitted by law.

Book Design: Wade Daughtry, Collectors Press, Inc.
Editor: Aimee Stoddard

Library of Congress Cataloging-in-Publication Data

Kimmerle, Beth, 1969-
    Candy : the sweet history / Beth Kimmerle.-- 1st American ed.
        p. cm.
Includes bibliographical references and index.
  ISBN 1-888054-83-2 (Hardcover : alk. paper)
  1. Candy. I. Title.
  TX791.K56 2003
  641.8'53--dc21

                                                    2003009588
Printed in China

9 8 7 6 5 4 3 2

Collectors Press books are available at special discounts for bulk purchases, premiums, and promotions. Special editions, including personalized inserts or covers, and corporate logos, can be printed in quantity for special purposes. For further information contact: Special Sales, Collectors Press, Inc., P.O. Box 230986 Portland, OR 97281. Toll free: 1-800-423-1848.

For a free catalog write:
Collectors Press, Inc.
P.O. Box 230986
Portland, OR 97281
Toll free: 1-800-423-1848
collectorspress.com

CONTENTS

FOREWORD

From a handful of M&M'S to a hand-dipped chocolate treat, candy has captivated the imagination of both children and adults for decades. My love of candy goes beyond the fact that it never fails to satisfy my sweet tooth. To me, the candy itself is an extraordinary art form. Its beauty lies in the vast combinations of colors, shapes, and textures.

The vibrant graphics used on candy packaging and advertising alone is a study in art history. At Dylan's Candy Bar, my partner Jeff Rubin and I showcase candy on backlit glass shelves to accentuate the wonderful packaging. Some of the most recognizable American icons are candy logos created decades ago and are still in use today. Beth Kimmerle pays proper homage to the artistry and creativity of candy packaging. In her book, *Candy: The Sweet History*, packaging graphics are displayed in their vintage color glory.

Old-fashioned candy has deep sentimental value. These treats remind us of simpler and more carefree times. Candy evokes memories of a time when life was more innocent and peaceful. From a pair of wax lips to a strand candy necklace, we all have a special place in our hearts for our favorite candy. Candy can make a hard day a little sweeter. Candy can also mark a tradition, like a fresh box of Junior Mints at the movies or homemade fudge at Christmas.

Like Charlie's excitement upon entering that famous Chocolate Factory, *Candy: The Sweet History* captures the enthusiasm of candy lovers and beautifully explains how candy is part of our American culture and heritage. I am honored to be a part of this book because Beth has an amazing and extensive knowledge about candy for which so many of us share a deep passion.

This book showcases our favorite candy as the art form and icon it truly is. So grab a handful of jellybeans, a box of Dots, or a Snickers Bar and take a sweet journey through these pages. But whatever you do — don't forget to share.

—Dylan Lauren, Owner, Dylan's Candy Bar

Pat-a-cake, pat-a-cake,
 candy man,
Buy Wrigley's Double Mint,
 fast as you can!
But as fast as you get it, the
 good people come
To get this delicious REAL
PEPPERMINT gum!
MOTHER GOOSE UP-TO-DATE.

Do you like a real, lasting, *built in*, full strength flavor REAL Peppermint?

Then get Wrigley's Double Mint at your dealers.

It is a new and better *Peppermint* flavor.

H79 ..."*After every meal!*"

A 1927 Wrigley ad featuring "Wrigley Arrows."
Courtesy Wrigley

After owning a small retail business for several years, I got a chance to work for a much larger business, a candy retailer and wholesaler. The company, Chicago-based Archibald Candy Co., is a huge corporation that had, at that time, been around for almost 80 years. I did something called Product Development. I designed, repackaged, bought, and sold all types of candy and confections for retail stores, catalogs, and other sales divisions. I got the job because of my retail experience, flavored with a bit of design background and because, like most people, I grew up on candy.

Candy was truly significant in my life. Like most kids, sweets played a central role in my childhood, and many memories orbit around candy. Birthday parties were special because the candy sanction was completely lifted. On road trips and car rides, candy usually made it into the back seat, probably as a silencing measure. Family movie outings usually permitted a visit to the candy counter. Even though we had to carve up a box of Non Pareils and Hot Tamales between us, after a bit of opposition, we did. Deacon's Dime Store, conveniently located around the block from one childhood home, saw many allowance cents. Mr. Deacon employed women who were as ancient as some of the inventory in the notions section. With their blue hair and bent fingers, they would quickly count out our penny candy on the counter and scoop it into a small brown bag perfectly built for a few Mary Janes, Smarties, Caramel Creams, Lemonheads, Tootsie Rolls, and a piece or two of Dubble Bubble. Halloween was unmistakably the holiday that brought in huge quantities of sweets. It served as a time to taste new treats, decide on favorites, and, of course, use candy as childhood currency. The peppermint forest and molasses swamp from Hasbro's Candyland game enchanted me the first time I entered them.

Apparently, I was more versed in the subject of sweets than I knew. During my second interview I could easily articulate tastes and packaging thoughts. My job was great; it came with many samples and a white lab coat. The coat had an embroidered patch with my name in cursive sewn on it. It hung in my office and usually had several balled-up hair nets stuffed in the pockets, necessary for my trips into the adjoining candy factory. There, I worked with designers along with box, paper, and film companies to create new packaging. I worked with in-house research and development teams mixing new tastes and flavors.

Often, when I needed a break, I would slip into the magical factory. After taking off all jewelry, because of metal restrictions, I would grab my customized coat and go. Sometimes I would visit Joe Labello in the hard candy room. Joe had worked in the factory for years. His room was always warm to keep the candy soft. A soft sugar mass left the room on a conveyer belt and was fed through a machine that molded it into various shapes and then cut it different lengths as it cooled. The finished product could be a delicately spun ribbon candy or a fluffy fruit-filled piece. Joe was calm and as sweet as the substance he worked with. His candy room was balmy and smelled fruity and fragrant. When the machines were running and I could sample a candy fresh off the line, somehow everything was okay.

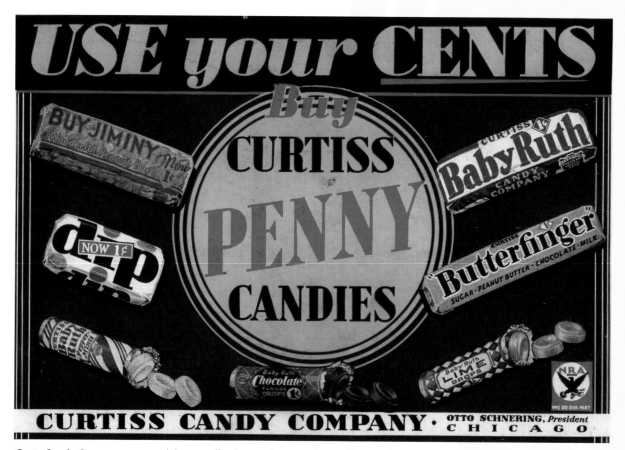

Curtis Candy Company supported the war effort by supplying candy to soldiers and in this 1940s advertisement encouraged consumers to use their sparse pennies to purchase their candies.

Archibald Candy Co. owns Fannie May and Fanny Farmer stores. Both are famous for their old-fashioned candy buttercreams and pieces like the delicious caramel and nut Pixie and the smooth, perfectly square Mint Meltaway. Many people can remember the paper-covered, one-pound candy boxes with the embossed cursive gold logo. The well-versed can identify the candy innards from the delicate swirl markings on the chocolate crest and can name their grandmother's favorite piece. Through my work there, I got a chance to know, appreciate, and develop a deep fascination for this sweet sector of business. As I learned the meaning of candy terms like panned and enrobed, I also became aware of the inside secrets of the candy business.

I was lucky to work with many other candy companies, buying their candy for the Fannie May and Fanny Farmer stores and catalogs. On my big, bulk-shopping list were jellybeans, sours, gummy bears, licorice, lollipops, and pectin fruit slices. I was invited to tour other factories to see how their goods were made. All companies did it differently. I have been in a few candy mills that had bar code scanners and electronic devices everywhere, making for a fast-paced, high-tech candy-building environment. The Jelly Belly factory had computer machines that formulated the different flavors and were run by scientists instead of workers like Joe LaBello. Still, other companies emphasized that their candy was still mostly handmade. I have been in a factory or two where I was astounded by the simplicity. A few ingredients, a few workers and straight away you have a candy! A factory tour is still fascinating to me today; I still feel a bit like Charlie Bucket when he won his golden ticket the moment I get an invitation.

It was while I toured a candy factory, an inner sugar sanctum, that it occurred to me that our love of candy is much more than a bodily reaction to sweets. It is also about getting a velvet heart-shaped box full of chocolate, batting piñatas filled with treats, reading *Charlie and the Chocolate Factory*, strolling the bountiful aisles of five-and-dimes, dressing up for Halloween, staring at filled racks at little corner drugstores, making necklaces from foil wrappers, collecting bubble gum cards and digging through cellophane grass to find the last jellybean. Candy is about memories.

No special event, occasion, or celebration is complete without candy. In fact, candy is considered a seasonal business with sales spikes hitting around big holidays like Christmas, Valentine's Day, and Easter. Many companies produce pieces specifically for holidays — think candy canes, Marshmallow Peeps, and Necco Conversation Hearts. Oh, and the chocolate Easter rabbit. I can clearly remember, one year, nestling my hollow, white chocolate Easter rabbit, decorated with a mini blue sugar eye, in a bookshelf reliquary next to my precious Hello Kitty stickers, a koala bear key chain and a puffy, rainbow-stuffed pillow. All were favorite items on display for complete adoration. Because chocolate rabbits were available only once a year, they always got royal treatment. This bunny was extra special as I had specifically asked the Easter Bunny for white chocolate instead of milk. I had newly discovered white chocolate and liked the fact that it would not get mixed up with the loot of my two sisters. There could be no "Oops — I ate your bunny by mistake!"

business this year from either my sisters or my parents. I remember sitting on my pink shag rug and watching the creamy white rabbit in the shrine while chewing on a marshmallow Peep or perhaps carefully sucking the coating off of a black jellybean. And when I was done honoring the rabbit and could not hold out any longer, I slowly ate it. But in my family, we never ever started with the head; we always started with the tail.

With no big holiday in the summer, candy companies use the time to breathe a sigh of relief before gearing up for Halloween. Most are happy not to ship their precious heat-vulnerable product in the sticky, hot weather. Anyone who's tasted a chocolate bar that has melted and then been cooled again will agree that candy is best factory fresh. Back in the day before air-conditioned trucks and cooler packs, many companies used the summer months to fix machinery and give their hard-working employees a break.

This whole candy business, I realized, was different than other industries, as many companies were still owned and operated by the families that started them. In addition, there was a camaraderie that seemed to be expiring in other American businesses. Over and over, I heard stories of amazing unity among what would seem like business competitors. For example, during WWII when sugar was rationed, some factories pooled their precious supplies. More recently, a Philadelphia-based company suffered a factory fire and received phone calls from neighboring candy producers offering machines to help keep production running. Not only did families run these individual candy producers, the candy business was one big household. The candy community is tight. Fathers have worked with fathers for years. Sons and daughters of the candy world have grown up together. I think today you'd be hard pressed to say this about many industries but the candy profession. Comprised of third, fourth, and fifth-generation, family-owned businesses that have worked together for years, the candy industry is a little old-fashioned and, dare I say, really sweet.

Originally called Kandy Kake, Otto Schnering thought his popular candy bar needed a new name. In a 1920s company contest, an employee suggested Baby Ruth, supposedly not for the Babe Ruth of baseball, but for the daughter of President Grover Cleveland.

Through wars, recessions, buy-outs, family turmoil, and sugar shortages, companies continued to produce their candy. I will profile the companies that were often started by immigrant entrepreneurs who came to the States with little money, often only a simple recipe and a huge sweet dream. Their homeland may have been Russia, Germany, or Armenia. The candy start-up stories were so similar. Time after time I heard, "My great-great grandfather came over to the States, started a modest, sweet-making production out of his home, almost lost the business once or twice during wars and depressions, and years later here we are, still making candy." The companies I will describe are still producing their signature candy pieces. They qualify as nostalgic as they have been around long enough for multiple generations to appreciate their product.

Some of these classic candy companies produce just one type of candy. They do that because that is what they do best. These are the candy companies that keep it simple. They might dabble in both milk and dark chocolate and the occasional seasonal wrapper but not much else. They have found a tasty formula and a trademark piece of candy and have stuck with it. These are companies like Doscher's Candy and Goetze. Doscher's makes the wonderfully classic French Chew taffy. Goetze started out in chewing gum along with a few other products before the firm began to concentrate solely on its famous caramel with the cream center or bull's-eye, as we called them back in the day. Both candy companies have been in business for over 100 years.

(L) A 1980s Wacky Wafer display box. Wacky Wafers, along with Nerds and Tart N Tiny, were Wonka Candy 1980s heavy hitters.
Michael Rosenberg Collection

(R) 1980s Lik-M-Aid Package. Lik-M-Aid, flavored sugar with a candy dipping stick, is now called Fun Dip and still a Wonka top seller.
Dan Goodsell Collection

Then there are the candy companies that produce a huge variety of different sweets. Some purchased smaller companies to widen their selection. Some expanded themselves to meet market needs. They may carry an assortment of wafers, bars, and taffy. Necco or New England Candy Company produces its famous Necco Wafer but also bought along the way the Clark Bar, Sky Bar, and Mary Jane to round out their classic offering. What these companies produce may vary but they all share something in common. They are unique American companies that continue to sell their product, not simply for great wealth but also for the love and tradition of it.

I do not mean to imply that there is not wealth involved in candy. Some of the bigger American candy companies like M&M Mars and Hershey are billion dollar companies, sending their sweet stuff all over the world. They allocate big dollars for new product marketing, character licensing, and research and development. But they have worked hard for their money and started out small like the rest. Both companies' founders had several failed candy businesses before they succeeded. Today, M&M Mars is still family-owned. Milton S. Hershey died one of the greatest American philanthropists, leaving his great wealth to an orphanage that now has a five-billion-dollar endowment. Both Hershey and Mars achieved the American dream.

At its high point, Curtiss Candy made everything from sweetened drink mix to chewing gum. This 1956 advertisement recommends candy around the calendar.

14

Because it's about simpler times and happy memories, nostalgic candy is hugely popular. Nostalgic candy can be big business not only for those who make the candy but also for those that sell it. A few savvy retailers have dedicated sweet-treat departments that sell our old-time favorites. In addition, websites like candyfavorites.com sell "hard-to-find" classic candies and have become big-dollar companies. Groovy Candy, one Internet favorite, regularly featured on TV, has taken all the great candies from the 1950s and the 1960s and assembled them into collections that "take you back in time."

High-end markets like Eli's and Citerella, both gourmet grocery merchants in New York City, carry nostalgic and hard-to-find American candy because, as one store manager said, "It is high quality, unique, and customers love to rediscover it." Some markets are cutting down on the once popular European imports, replacing them with the less-common but widely loved American product. I was surprised to see that the Valomilk Candy Cup made it to New York from Kansas City. For the most part, that particular candy is distributed primarily around the area where it is manufactured. With beautiful packaging that hasn't changed in years and a delicious, yet fragile flowing marshmallow center, this nostalgic candy is hard to ship, hard to find, so discovering it in New York is a total candy score.

New York's popular Dylan's Candy Bar, located directly behind the New York shopping mecca Bloomingdales, offers a majestic assortment of nostalgic novelty candy. Dylan Lauren and Jeff Rubin present items such as the Necco Wafer, Clark Bar, Sugar Daddy, Nik-L-Nip, and vintage Pez collections. In addition to candy, Dylan's offers a selection of candy-festooned clothing with iconic Mr. Lemonhead and Hot Tamale designs. Downstairs, along with their large section of classic candies, they feature a candy history timeline and an enclosed glass showcase area exhibiting a candy museum. The museum displays old candy artifacts, wrappers, and boxes that are fun to check out. Their collection of old-time boxes and wrappers make the many spectators smile.

Nostalgic candy also has a starring and reoccurring role on TV. The top rated *Unwrapped* series from the Food Network "reveals the magic and secrets of America's best-loved food and drink." *Unwrapped* has programs about classic American foods such as candy corn, chocolate syrup, cotton candy, and bubble gum. *Unwrapped* explores the test kitchens and the secrets behind lunchbox treats, soda pop, and movie candy. *Unwrapped* is touted as the show for everyone "who's ever worn a pair of wax lips."

1946 candy wholesale
catalog advertisement.
Dan Goodsell collection

Wouldn't *you* like some candy?

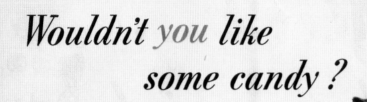

If you were an engineer on a famous train and you had checked over everything for the run and you had a few minutes to relax and refresh, wouldn't *you* like some candy?

If you were a fast-ball pitcher and the game was close and you had to keep bearing down hard and energy was starting to wane, when you came back to the dugout wouldn't *you* like some candy?

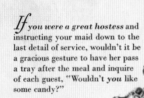

If you were a great hostess and instructing your maid down to the last detail of service, wouldn't it be a gracious gesture to have her pass a tray after the meal and inquire of each guest, "Wouldn't *you* like some candy?"

If you were a high school grad and on the romance road in high gear wouldn't it be nice to open the evening with "Wouldn't *you* like some candy?"

It's true.. Most everybody likes Candy!

IN BOX

IN BAR

IN BAG

CANDY IS DELICIOUS FOOD

Enjoy same every day!

COUNCIL ON CANDY of the **NATIONAL CONFECTIONERS' ASSOCIATION**...One North La Salle Street, Chicago 2, Illinois

© 1947—NCA   ...an organization devoted to the dissemination of authoritative information about candy

This 1947 National Confectioners' Association confirms it is indeed true: candy is simply perfect for all occasions.
Beth Kimmerle Collection

Nostalgic candy is so very American. The nostalgic Americana as a trend is popular in products, along with remembering simpler times and small treats from the corner store. Americana memories sell, especially in complicated political and economic times. Candy, it has been said, is almost recession-proof because it is an item that, for a small cost, helps people feel better. Retailers do well in general with "yesteryear" theme products, from vintage toys and nostalgic holiday decorations to the best in hard-to-find classic goodies. Today, generations have candy in common. A Snickers bar today is much like the Snickers from 1929 when it was launched. Packages can change slightly but candy remains a great timeless, familiar treat.

Vintage candy memorabilia and ephemera are highly collectible. On the auction website eBay, thousands of American candy jars, wrappers, dishes, and boxes are top-sellers. Items like old candy display boxes and penny candy jars from old-fashioned candy stores bring top dollar. Vendors at street fairs hawk high-priced old Hershey's display signs, Wrigley gum racks, Wacky Packages stickers, and Pez dispensers. When I see what the Wacky Packages stickers fetch, I wish I had not stuck them all over the side of my desk when I was nine.

When I mention old-time candy favorites to friends, they respond immediately and enthusiastically. Candy has positive connotations and brings back intense emotional recollections. Candy is usually the first item bought (and the first stolen from the Woolworth's), and the first food item that people consume, think about, and crave. Candy is the item of choice for school fundraisers. Kids quickly become experts and specialists in their favorites. People choose candy that has popular and trendy flavors but also choose candy for the toys, packaging, and play factor attached. Many toys today are part toy, part candy, and part spinning something. But the classic treats, like the trading cards, Bazooka gum wrapped in a cartoon, and Pez, offered something to taste and added something simple to play with, which made them very popular.

The business of candy is not just for kids — many adults still consume it and remember their favorite sweets vividly. Power protein bars, in my opinion, are just repackaged adult candy. In fact, for many years, candy companies talked about the health benefits of candy. In their ads, they claimed candy "supplied energy with fresh essential ingredients." In the 1930s, Curtis Candy had a character, featured on their Baby Ruth packaging, with the letters NRG ("energy") on his sweater. The cartoon character, through his Curtiss Candy bullhorn, talked of dextrose being a great fuel for the body. The wrapper also had an "Accepted by the American Medical Association" seal proudly displayed in a corner.

Curtiss Candy promoted good health and dextrose intake with their mascot, "NRG".
Beth Kimmerle Collection

Many of my friends keep a secret stash in the office drawer or sit close to a vending machine. Hardware stores and office supply stores have a not-so-little candy section these days. On my first visit to the afore-mentioned Dylan's Candy, I witnessed some parents showing more candy excitement than their children. One woman held up a Chic-O-Stick and laughed while junior looked baffled by the orange candy. I was at a party and a glass of wine reminded someone of a certain candy. Eagerly we smelled it and passed it around until someone identified the exact piece and flavor. The white wine tasted remarkably similar to a green-apple-flavored Jolly Rancher. Some can even remember the vivid sound and feeling of unfolding a wrapper or splitting a piece with their back teeth to share with a friend. The sight of nostalgic candy evokes joy and excitement in voices and eyes. Many times I have heard, "Whatever happened to...," and, "Do they still make...?"

Mention marshmallow Peeps, taffy, and licorice and you'll understand that candy is a very passionate topic. I think perhaps candy is the first item that we feel loyal to. I can remember having my favorites; I was not really interested in possibly wasting my hard earned allowance by trying a new candy. I stuck by my candy then and still have my favorites now. I can never seem to resist a piece of black licorice. Good and Plenty, vine, or rope and especially a fresh jellybean — licorice is my favorite.

A Brach's full service candy counter from a 1960 advertisement. Brach's Candy started with a small Chicago shop in 1908. By 1958, Brach's Pic-A-Mix was featured in national supermarkets and allowed customers to purchase their favorite bulk candy by the pound.

This book takes a look at the candy companies that have been around for a while, continuing to make the candy that makes us happy. It is the candy that has joined us at birthday parties and movies for many years. I am telling their stories because these founders lived the American dream and they are a part of American history. Their classic candy packaging has become iconic. This book about American candy is my homage to these great nostalgic candy companies and an acknowledgement of their effort to carry on a tasty tradition. This book is a place for them to show off their best stuff and leave their legacy.

Lastly, it is a book to help all of us to remember the sweet things in our lives.

A sparkling Loft's candy store-, shown here in 1959 when the company had over 200 East Coast stores.

THE HISTORY OF CANDY

CHAPTER 1

At its most basic, candy is a very simple thing. For example, a hard candy is simply sugar dissolved in water with flavoring and color added. The word candy refers to numerous confections — both soft and hard — that are made of sugar that has been cooked. Different heating and cooling levels determine types of candy: hot temperatures make hard candy, medium heat makes soft candy, and cooler temperatures make a chewy candy. The temperature difference between fudge and a caramel is only a few degrees on the candy thermometer. So while candy is formed with simple ingredients, exact heating levels make the production of candy scientific.

Mixing simple sugar candies with other flavors and textures such as fruits, spices, coconut, nuts, or chocolate make it more complex. The sweet possibilities are really limitless.

American candy makers have explored every taste combination over the years. To sell and market their products, they have been equally creative with names and packaging. Crunchy peanut butter and toasted coconut shaped to look like a slender chicken leg, called a Chic-O-Stick, has been a favorite since the 1930s. Milk chocolate, caramel, peanuts, and marshmallow, called a Goo Goo Cluster and named after a baby's first words, was the first combination candy bar. America's oldest operating candy company produces Necco Wafers, multicolored wafers punched from pulverized paste and nestled in glassy vellum. The lively candy concoction list goes on.

Candy, however, is hardly an American invention. Humans have been chomping on sweets for thousands of years. It is documented that early Homo sapiens enjoyed fresh honey from beehives. It seems that they also extracted sweet saps from trees. Chewy sap, sometimes combined with beeswax, was used to form the earliest chewing gum and has been found in ancient tombs and referred to in early writings.

As cultures became more sophisticated, so did their sweetmeats. During ancient times, the Egyptians, Arabs, and Chinese were known to prepare sweet confections of fruit and nuts candied in honey. The dried fruits and nuts were prepared by mixing in sweet, spicy, or floral ingredients. Licorice has been used as a natural sweetener and herbal healer for centuries. Dates and figs, naturally high-sugar fruits, enhanced early sweets with their juices. However, it was bees' honey that remained the main sweetener until sugar was traded outside its natural terrain.

Sugar or sucrose is extracted from a thick reed stalk. The giant grass, sugar cane, hails from India and is mentioned in ancient Sanskrit texts from 1200 B.C. A popular Persian delicacy, a sweet reed flavored with honey and spices, was called "kand." The Arab word for sugar is "qand." Perhaps both are early derivations of the word candy. For years, sugar was traded throughout the Middle East, but it didn't leave that region until the Crusaders discovered the "sweet salt" on their conquests.

Sugar spread to Europe sometime in the 11th century once the Crusaders returned from their travels. Impressed with the exotic sweetened drinks and fruits they found abroad, they created a demand once they landed back home. As sugarcane became available, its high cost made consuming confections and sweets a delicacy accessible only to the wealthy. Like other spices that were imported and traded into Europe, it was prized and often used in conspicuous extravagances by those who could afford it.

By the 13th century, Venice was the sugar capital of the world. Decorative sugar sculptures became the rage for European royalty and their courts. Candy as an art was developed by royal, court-appointed confectioners who were encouraged to explore the decadent possibilities of the exotic substance. The highly regarded confectioners often presented lavish table decorations for a final course. The theatrical centerpieces were made from molded sugar paste and were served along with spun sugar baskets containing prized dragees and candied fruit for take-home treats. Beginning a long tradition of giving sultry sweets at parties and weddings.

Apart from the copious decor, sugar was primarily used to preserve fruits, nuts, and flowers. Fruits lasted for weeks when cooked and coated with sugar. Citrus rinds sweetened deliciously when boiled in sugar. Flowers like violets and miniature roses were candied and eaten. Candied nuts, called confetti or Jordan almonds, are still given today at ceremonies to represent fertility. Sugar, the stored food from a plant much like a fat in an animal, brought out the natural sweetness in fresh products and transformed them into delicacies.

Because of its sweet taste, sugar was also used widely in medicines. Apothecaries coated their bitter herbal remedies with sugar in order to mask the unpleasant tastes. They also prescribed sugar itself for ailments like dry lips, chest pains, and stomach turmoil. It was a pharmacy staple and was sold as a substance with multiple healing properties.

With the introduction of cocoa and coffee to the world, the demand for sugar grew. Sugar perfectly complimented and offset the bitterness of both the coffee and cocoa beans. All three became commodities and their popularity and marketability gave European countries motive to colonize islands and tropical areas where the fashionable substances grew best. The Portuguese grew sugar in Brazil and by 1570 had almost 75 plantations devoted to sugar production. From the 16th to the 18th centuries, sugar cane spread around the world. By the 17th century, Amsterdam had over 1000 refineries and became the center of sugar trade. The growth and spread of sugar allowed the ingredient to be enjoyed by many. It has been noted, however, that this substance brought much sorrow for something so sweet. Workers were needed to fuel the plantations where these new exotic ingredients were grown and processed. Ships sailed from refineries loaded with sugar by-products like rum and molasses, returning later with human resources. It is certain that the slaves who were responsible for growing and refining sugar, cocoa, and coffee never got to taste their enthralling flavors.

The Spanish introduced cocoa to Europe from South America in the 1400s. With the introduction of cocoa to Europe, a whole new confection world opened up. Aztecs drank the bitter cocoa as a thick and frothy drink spiced with vanilla and chili peppers. Cocoa was consumed at many Aztec ceremonies and rituals. Chocolate was taken before heading into battle. The spices gave it a deep red color, and often warriors wore it intentionally around their mouths to simulate blood. The Mayans consumed chocolate earlier, perhaps as early as 500 A.D. Theobroma Cacao, the cacao tree fruit's scientific name, literally means food of the gods. Cocoa beans were treated as little treasures, used in trade and as currency.

As some candy hoarders will, Spanish monks did their best to hide the secret of cocoa making for close to 100 years. But soon, news of the unusual beverage leaked beyond the monastery and King Ferdinand's court walls. The first English chocolate houses opened in 1657. Cocoa remained a bitter, unsweetened drink that was heated and served with cinnamon. Cocoa was mostly reserved for the rich and royalty and would not be regularly sweetened with sugar and milk until more than a hundred years later.

When candies originally met cocoa, it did not seem they had much in common. But as they moved from luxury items to the mainstream, that would change. Production of both sugar and cocoa increased and therefore prices decreased, allowing more people to enjoy them. Slowly, chocolate appeared in cakes and pastries. Even with cheaper prices, only the simple boiled-sugar hard candies were enjoyed by most in 17th century in England and in the American colonies.

It did not take long for early confectioners to start mixing all the luscious ingredients together to make chocolate candy. Sweet making developed rapidly into an industry during the early 19th century after the discovery of natural fruit and vegetable juice sweeteners from products like beets and grapes. The advance of mechanical equipment was also a force in creating candy commerce. With the industrial revolution, many industries advanced as a result of new efficiencies and technologies. Homemade hard candies, such as peppermints and lemon drops, became popular and widely available in America during that time. The upper class had a wider choice of pastilles, gumdrops, bonbons, and candied ginger.

Molded hard candy — decorative as well as sweet — was some of the first candy that was mass-produced.

In 1828, a Dutch chocolatier named Conrad J. van Houton created a process of pressing a large amount of fat or cocoa butter from the cocoa bean. By extracting some of the fat content, the cocoa could be sold in a powder or cake form. His discovery gave future chocolatiers and confectioners the ability to easily flavor any creation, not just drinks. With Houton's process, "Dutched" chocolate could easily be added to liquids and powders.

By the mid 1800s, more than 380 American factories were producing penny candy. Most of the confections were sold by weight. These sweet pieces were sold loose from glass cases, boxes, and jars. Candy was available at local general stores, and pharmacies still carried cough drops and sweet syrups, candy's original cousins. In more urban areas, roadside candy companies started with a cooking or panning kettle in the back kitchen and a small "retail" room in the front. These storefronts became the first candy shops.

By the 1850s, accessible candies shifted from simple hard candies to fudges and chocolate-coated pieces. Mass-produced and distributed, hard and soft candies became widely available. Some of these first mass-produced candies had extra "health benefits." These curative American candies were known to soothe throats and ease headaches, often with medicinal additives like cocaine and heroin mixed right into the sugar.

The early steam engine allowed machinists to produce the first candy-making machines. Even today, a revolving steam pan is a vital piece of equipment for some manufacturers. Steam also offers a consistent way to cook the very unstable sugar.

With candy companies manufacturing more candy, inventive packaging was introduced. In 1868, Richard Cadbury packaged his candies in a heart shaped box, introducing the first box of Valentine's Day chocolates. By the 1870s, many candies were beginning to be sold in elaborate bottles and boxes, packed up for easy distribution and freshness. Packaging gave companies an opportunity to spread their names, broaden their brands, and distinguish their product. The fancy candy box added another dimension to candy by offering the consumer an ornate souvenir object that could later hold love letters and special keepsakes.

Candy, because of its glorious and regal background, had always been a symbolic component of special occasions, courting, and holidays. Words that described the taste of candy such as sweetie, sugar, and honey were becoming terms of affection.

Still in the early confection years, chocolate was not viewed as a necessary ingredient in candy making. It was mostly still enjoyed as a drink or candy coating until 1876 when Daniel Peter of Vevey, Switzerland, invented a way to make solid milk chocolate. He added condensed milk, made by Henry Nestle, to the chocolate liquor, thereby creating milk chocolate. Later his fellow countryman, Rudolphe Lindt, developed a processing that gave the chocolate a silky texture as a result of conching or mixing the chocolate.

Thousands save on lunch this tasty way

They know their Baby Ruth

Here's a real way to make your lunches more delightful, and save money too: eat Baby Ruth for dessert. It's delicious and satisfying. A generous tasty treat of dollar-a-pound quality candy for five cents.

Daily, thousands are finding it the most enjoyable dessert they can buy.

Because it is made of purest chocolate, nuts, milk and sugar, dietitians say Baby Ruth makes a light lunch more invigorating than a heavier meal—that it supplies all the extra energy you need for hard work and play. Because you eat less and feel better, it's a healthful way to control your weight.

Baby Ruth is famous for flavor and *guaranteed fresh*. Treat yourself at lunch today. 5c does it.

CURTISS
Baby Ruth
America's Favorite Candy 5¢

© 1928. C. C. Co.

In dainty slices — the popular guest candy of today

CURTIS
CANDY COMPANY, CHICA
OTTO SCHNERING, President
Also makers of Baby Ruth Gum "with that old time Peppermint

MADE IN BILLIONS FOR AMERICA'S MILLIO

During the Depression, candy was marketed as a wholesome meal replacement for the many who were unable to afford a proper meal.

Milton S. Hershey realized those Swiss were on to something. During a trip to Europe, the "caramel king" gathered information that would lead him to purchase innovative chocolate equipment at Chicago's Colombian Exposition in 1893. Milton Hershey produced his first chocolate bars the following year. Shortly after, he sold his profitable Lancaster Caramel Company in order to work exclusively in chocolate. By 1905, Hershey was producing the first mass produced milk chocolate bar.

By the turn of the 20th century, when America gained new candy technology and displayed at World Fairs, there were more than 1,000 different candy producers. Candy bar machines, chocolate enrobers, and basic candy refrigeration equipment were unveiled for both the public and the daring entrepreneurs to behold. Small local companies were making bars, Non Pareils, drops, pastels, licorice, caramel, taffy, marshmallow, and gums in a variety of shapes and flavors.

The growing candy business remained mostly seasonal, with the Christmas season being the busiest. This worked out well, for in the summer months it was not only hard to ship candy but unbearable to work in hot factories without air conditioning. Large-scale candy making involved both cooking and hauling mixtures in large vats and batches. Making candy was labor intensive. The candy factory kitchens were often shut down for maintenance and repair during the slow summer months. Candy factory workers could enjoy a much deserved break.

The candy business was attractive to many new immigrants to America. A simple candy operation was relatively easy to set up. Many candy pieces could be made by hand, with machinery added when business blossomed. Family members were put to work making and distributing candy and sometimes working in the family candy store. Candy was also a way for immigrant families to connect with one another, share their recipes, and remember flavors from home.

The combination candy bar, a bar comprised of several ingredients, was developed in 1912. It was first sold wrapped and ready to eat at baseball games. While a few companies take credit for inventing this delicious treat, Standard Candy Company's Goo Goo Cluster was near the front.

The candy bar became widely known with World War I when manufacturing methods were updated to accommodate orders from U.S. soldiers serving overseas. Hershey formulated a heat resistant "D Ration" bar. The daily ration bar was an introduction to Hershey products for many soldiers and Europeans alike. The U.S. Army gave candy companies important contracts at a time when vital candy-making supplies like butter and cocoa were rationed. After the war, soldiers came home calling for the convenient and tasty candy that they had met overseas. The 1920s was a booming time for bars, with as many as 40,000 candy bars in production!

Daniel Peter perfected a way to form solid milk chocolate by adding Nestlé's condensed milk. His discovery helped shift the public's preference from chocolate drink to candy bar.
Nestlé's Collection

Oh, you Candy Kid.

Turn-of-the-century postcard depicting candy and romance.

1920s 'Tween Meals candy wrapper.
Courtesy Chase and Poe Candy Company

Macke Vending Company 1960 annual report.

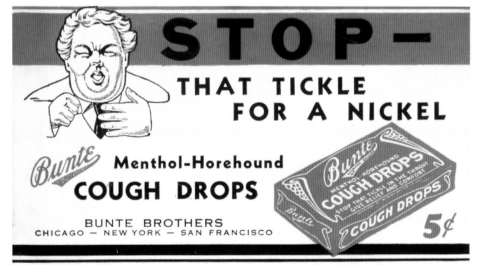

Just a spoonful of sugar…Cough drops and candy are linked, as sugar was used to mask the unpleasant tastes of early medicines.

Candy products helped feed the masses during the Depression. Candy was often peddled as a satisfying and healthy meal substitute, and bars called Chicken Dinner, Tummy Full, and Denver Sandwich lined shelves and had a square-meal ring to them. Candy companies that could afford it, lowered prices to stimulate sales and stay in business.

Candy came home to a hero's welcome after World War II. For years, Americans had lived through sugar shortages and rations and couldn't get their fix of candy. Many companies had stopped production for lack of supplies and ingredients. Some companies had converted manufacturing space to assembly lines for the military. As confectioners went back to making their sweets, lines formed at the shops with the latest supply of gum and candy. Because of the vital role it played in energizing soldiers, candy got an image boost and was viewed as a healthy necessity instead of an indulgence.

Candy prices shot from five cents to ten cents in 1964 and signaled the end of a sweet era. The boutique companies that were able to thrive during the candy boom years were consolidating or going out of business. Candy selections were smaller and less regional. Candy, like other businesses, was starting to homogenize, nationalize, and taste the same.

Today, Americans still have a collective sweet tooth; the average person consumes 12 pounds of sugar-candy product each year. While there are not as many individual candy producers, if you look hard, there is still an amazing array and selection of candy on the market.

Candy graces aisles and the prime real estate of drugstores, convenience stores, supermarkets, and the local deli. Today, candy is big business. In the year 2002, candy, chocolate, and gum sales were over $24 billion dollars. The big candy companies, with their marketing dollars and budgets, make it tough on smaller companies. Smaller candy companies are left to distribute to mom-and-pop stores or simply go out of business. Cities like Chicago and Boston, once manufacturing meccas for small and mid-size confection companies, are losing factories to big companies and consolidation. Back in that day, candy was king in those cities. They were conveniently close to fresh products such as cream and butter and could ship quickly from existing transportation hubs. However, candy is now a global treat, and competing in that market is tough on the small, family-owned candy business. Sugar, manufacturing, and labor are all less expensive in other parts of the world.

The list of candy that is no longer available grows, as does the need to celebrate the candy that is still available. It is these classic American candies that really take people back the simple time when life was all about a bag of penny candy from the five-and-dime. There is nothing quite like unwrapping a remembered sweet and experiencing a delicious taste from the past.

CHAPTER 2

1868

Richard Cadbury introduces the first Valentine's Day box of chocolates.

1871

Doscher's Confections opens in Cincinnati, later producing their taffy French Chew.

1876

G.W. Chase starts his business that later becomes Chase Candy Company.

1893

William Wrigley, Jr., introduces Juicy Fruit Gum and Wrigley's Spearmint Gum.

1895

August Goetze begins producing confections and gum. He later concentrates on the perennial favorite Goetze Caramel Cream.

1896

Introduced by Leo Hirshfield of New York, Tootsie Rolls debut. Hirshfield named them after his daughter whose nickname was "Tootsie."

1898

Goelitz Confectionery Company begins making candy corn or "chicken feed." The firm continues to make this Halloween favorite longer than any other company.

1900

Milton S. Hershey of Lancaster, Pennsylvania, introduces the first Hershey milk chocolate bar. The 5-cent bar introduces chocolate to the masses, revolutionizing chocolate forever.

American Candy starts producing candy. The company later specializes in wax novelties like lips, fangs, and Nik-L-Nips.

Pastel-colored candy disks called NECCO wafers first appear. They are named for the acronym of the New England Confectionery Company.

1901

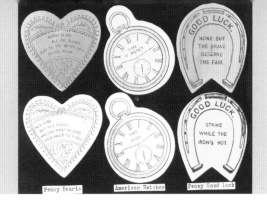

1902

NECCO makes the first conversation hearts — tiny Valentine's Day favorites with messages printed on them.

The Squirrel Brand Company of Massachusetts creates the first peanut bar. Soon, the company also produces the Squirrel Nut Zipper taffy.

1905

Gimbal Brother Candy Company miraculously survives the San Francisco earthquake.

Hershey's Kisses appear in their now-familiar foil wraps.

1906

Idaho Candy builds a modern factory to produce the now cult favorite Idaho Spud Bar.

1909

1912

Life Savers, the candy named for its ring shape with the hole in the center, is introduced in peppermint flavor. It is 22 years before the popular five-flavor roll is introduced.

1913

Goo Goo Clusters, a Southern favorite, becomes the first bar to combine milk chocolate, caramel, marshmallow, and peanuts.

American Licorice produces its first black licorice candies, later creating Red Vines.

1914

Palmer Candies converts its transportation from horse-drawn wagons to modern motorized trucks.

1917

Hammond's Candy of Denver creates recipes for ribbon candy and lollipops still in use today.

Fannie May Candies opens its first candy shop in Chicago. It produces a variety of chocolate-enrobed buttercreams and caramels.

The Baby Ruth candy bar is first sold. It is named for President Grover Cleveland's daughter, not the famous baseball player.

1922

Goldenberg's Peanut Chews are first made in Philadelphia and soon become popular along the East Coast.

Mounds, the double candy bar, is first made. It offers a coconut filling covered in chocolate.

1923

M&M Mars Milk Way bar is the first of many candies to be introduced by the Mars family.

1924

Bit-O-Honey debuts, the honey-flavored taffy
bar made with bits of almond.

1925

Milk Duds are introduced as bite-size caramel morsels covered in chocolate.

1926

1927

Cleve Gilliam opens his candy business. Gilliam Candy now
produces classic taffy favorites – BB Bats, Kits, and Slo Pokes.

Crunchy Heath Bars appear, offering chocolate-covered toffee.

Walter Diemer, an accountant for Fleer Gum, invents Dubble Bubble while experimenting in the factory.

Walt Diemer
29 years

1928

Reese's Peanut Butter Cups, named for the man who created them, debut. They are among the most popular candy bars today.

1929

M&M Mars introduces the Snickers Bar, named for a favorite horse owned by the Mars family. It's consistently the number-one selling candy bar in the United States.

Tootsie Roll Pops are introduced and soon become widely advertised as the lollipop that offers two candies in one — flavored hard candy on the outside and chewy Tootsie Roll center inside.

1931

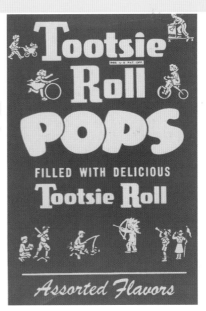

Valomilk, the creamy marshmallow-center candy cup, is developed by accident in Sifer's candy factory.

1931

Atkinson Candy, makers of Chick-O-Stick, begin production in Texas. Red Hots are made by Ferrara Pan Candy Company. These fiery little candy pellets are flavored with cinnamon.

1932

M&M Mars debuts the 3 Musketeers bar, originally made as a three-flavor bar featuring chocolate, vanilla, and strawberry nougat. In 1945, it is changed to all-chocolate nougat.

1933

1934

Charles Howard sells his first violet mints. Their scent attracts customers, requesting the floral favorite, to his SoHo factory door.

Boyer Candy Company moves to a bigger factory as their Mallo Cup takes off.

1935

The 5th Avenue bar is developed by the man perhaps best known for his cough drops — William H. Luden. The bar is made from layers of peanut butter crunch coated in milk chocolate.

1936

1937

Ben Myerson, after years at Hoffman's Candy, starts his own business, later creating Good News and Big Cherry bars.

Hershey's Miniatures chocolate bars debut. **1939**

M&M's Plain Chocolate Candies are introduced in response to slack chocolate sales in summer. **1940**

Junior Mints offer candies with soft mint centers drenched in dark chocolate.

1949

Smarties small, pastel candy disks are introduced, followed by the Smarties Necklace nine years later.

El Bubble Bubble Gum Cigars are the first 5-cent bubble gum. In the mid-1980s, the same company begins to make pink and blue bubble gum cigars to celebrate births.

Annabelle Candy Company starts. They go on to make classics such as Rocky Road, Abba Zaba, Big Hunk, Look!, and U-NO candies.

1950

Eyepatch-wearing Bazooka Joe first appears in Topps Comics.

1953

Marshmallow Peeps, in the shape of Easter chicks, are introduced by Just Born, Inc. Today, more than 2 million Peeps are made each day.

1954

Pearson Candy Company celebrates its 50th birthday. The Salted Nut Roll and Nut Goodie bar become traditional favorites.

1959

1960

M&M Mars Starburst Fruit Chews are introduced, fortified with 50 percent of the daily value for Vitamin C.

Blammo becomes the first sugar-free, soft bubble gum introduced by Amurol Confections.

1962

Lemonheads are created by Ferrara Pan Candy Company, later inspiring a series of fruit-flavored, panned candies.

1963

SweeTarts, the candy with the original sweet and tart flavor combination, are introduced.

1974

M&M Mars Skittles bite-size candies are introduced.

Introduced by Herman Goelitz Candy Company, Jelly Belly Jelly Beans offer consumers fun and unique flavors in a tiny jellybean.

1976

Hershey's Reese's Pieces bite-size candies are introduced and four years later made popular by the blockbuster movie E.T.

Spangler Candy adds the Saf-T-Pop to their line up that includes Dum Dum, Astro Pop, and candy canes.

1978

Makers of Jelly Bellies, Goelitz introduces the first American-made gummy bears and gummy worms. Formerly, these candies were imported from Europe.

1980

Ce De Candy, makers of Smarties, appoint Mr. T to help promote their product.

1991

Blitz Power Mints are one of several strong mints introduced in the 1990s as the breath freshener category grows.

1994

Holopops become the first hologram lollipops introduced by Light Vision Confections. The design on their etched surface appears to change as you move the pop.

1998

1999

Sound Bites Lollipops from Cap Candies is the first radio-lollipop combination in the growing interactive candy segment.

Tootsie Roll celebrates is 100th anniversary of being listed on the New York Stock Exchange, while producing more than 60 million Tootsie Rolls and 20 million Tootsie Pops each day.

2001

2003

Jelly Belly Candy Company introduces JBz, milk chocolate pieces covered with Jelly Belly top tastes like Buttered Popcorn, Honey Graham Cracker, Toasted Marshmallow, and Very Cherry!

BLUEBERRY

APRICOT

GRAPE

RASPBERRY

SIZZLING CINNAMON

GREEN APPLE

STRAWBERRY CHEESECAKE

ORANGE JUICE

TUTTI-FRUITTI

LICORICE

BUTTERED POPCORN

CAPPUCCINO

COCONUT

COTTON CANDY

TOASTED MARSHMALLOW

ICE BLUE MINT

JUICY PEAR

HONEY GRAHAM CRACKER

VERY CHERRY

TOP BANANA

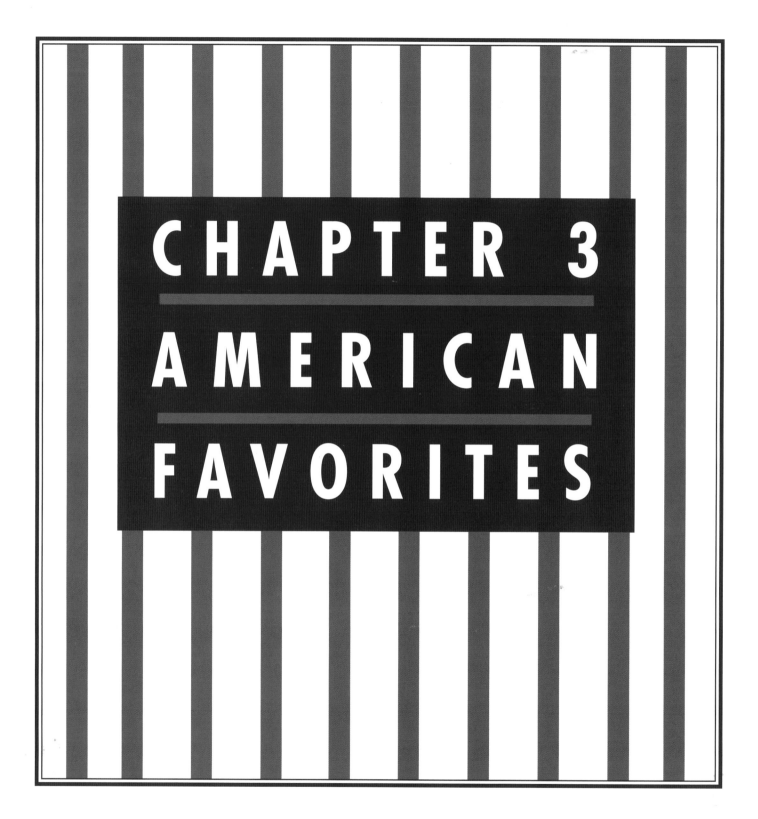

CHAPTER 3
AMERICAN FAVORITES

JELLY CANDY

The jelly family ranges from soft and tender to gummy and chewy. Today's jelly candies are direct descendants of Turkish Delight, which dates back to the Ottoman Empire. Early Turkish Delight was a combination of honey, roses, and jasmine bound with gum Arabic. Now jelly candies are made by adding pectin and starch to the sugar mix to create textures and bright colors. Pectin is a natural, water-soluble substance found in apples and citrus. It is used for its thickening properties in the preparation of jams and candies. Pectin-based jelly candies tend to be soft and chewy with fruit jelly centers. Jelly Beans, some of the more popular jelly candies, have been an Easter tradition since the 1930s. Gummy bears, gumdrops, and fruit slices are other examples of jelly candies.

America's most popular jelly candy

Chuckles

CHUCKLES

5 CHUCKLES

5 FLAVORS

cherry
lemon
licorice
orange
lime

5 CENTS

Nationally advertised to reach millions

NWCA MERCHANDISER Insert No. 1-15

Dan Goodsell Collection

LICORICE

Everybody Likes Switzer's Licorice

PACKED
16—6 BAR PACKAGES
TO SHIPPING CASE

SWITZER'S TAKE HOME PACKAGE

Millions of people have eaten
Hundreds of Millions
of Switzer's Bars

Recognized as the Nation's
Leading Licorice Bar

Nationally Advertised in

SWITZER'S LICORICE CO., ST. LOUIS, MO.

NCWA MERCHANDISER INSERT NO. 1-17

Dan Goodsell Collection

A candy flavored with the oil extract of a European or Asian root plant. This ancient flavoring is one of the oldest known; it has been used for centuries to flavor sweets, drinks, medicine, and other foods. Incredibly sweet, licorice extract is naturally 50 times sweeter than sucrose or sugar. Licorice is known to have beneficial healing properties. Licorice flavors candy ropes, gum, twists, hard candies, and pastels.

Licorice is mentioned in the 5,000-year-old Chinese herbal guide the Pen Tsao Ching and is still one of China's most popular herbs. Today it is prescribed for coughs, ulcers, respiratory problems, malaria, liver complaints, and cancers.

An English pharmacist, George Dunhill, who wanted to stretch his supply of pure licorice root, started using licorice to flavor candy in 1760. He added sugar and flour to extend it, producing a soft and sweet candy. The product was a success, and the candy company is still in existence.

TAFFY

Taffy is a soft and chewy, boiled-sugar candy that is pulled until porous. It is often colored and flavored. Taffy is made with molasses, butter, and brown sugar. Its supple consistency is achieved by pulling the candy into long strands as it cools. The thick taffy ropes are then usually cut into bite-size pieces and rolled into wax paper twists.

Saltwater taffy gained popularity around the turn of the century on the Atlantic City boardwalk. Pastel-colored taffy soon spread to other seaside communities and was associated with ocean vendors. But it was not named for the fresh salt air that would mist the candy. Saltwater taffy was named simply because the recipe calls for a small amount of salt water in the mixture. The British version of taffy, called toffy, is slightly harder than America's version.

NOUGAT

Popular in Europe, particularly France, Spain, and Italy, this confection was originally made of roasted nuts and candied fruit cooked in honey and ground into a paste. The Arabs are reputed to have introduced almond nougat to Spain. Now, many countries have their own regional versions.

Torrone, as it is called in Italy, is a traditional Italian candy, with a history dating from ancient Roman times. Montelimar, France, is famous for nougat. Its well-known legend tells of a kind old woman who would make candy of honey, eggs and nuts for the neighborhood children. They thanked her for her candy, saying, "Tu nous gates." You spoil us.

Today, nougat is a sweet made from honey, almonds or pistachios, candied fruit, and beaten egg whites. It is still served for special occasions, weddings, and celebrations. It can be chewy or hard and ranges from pure white to dark brown. Darker nougat is colored with brown sugar or chocolate and is often firmer in texture.

CARAMEL

Invented by the Arabs, the first caramel was burnt sugar. Harem ladies used it not as a sweet but as a hair remover. Caramel is produced when sugar has been cooked or caramelized. It is heated to between 320-350 degrees and becomes a thick liquid that can range in color from golden to deep brown. Adding different amounts of vanilla, corn syrup, butter, and milk can produce a sticky, brown, delectable confection. Caramel is used in desserts and as a topping. When cool, it is the base for brittle.

MARSHMALLOW

**DIPPING MARSHMALLOWS—
MARSHMALLOW SHEET**

"The Candy Maker's Friend." Real egg marshmallows with correct "body" to withstand the heat of dipping or candy making.

**HEAVY
GUM MARSHMALLOWS**

**LONG DIPPING
MARSHMALLOWS**

**LARGE ROUND DIPPING M. M.
SMALL ROUND DIPPING M. M.**

**SMALL WAFER
MARSHMALLOWS**

MARSHMALLOW SHEET

LACOOM SHEET

A spongy, sweet confection made of corn syrup, gelatin or egg white, sugar, and starch and set with powdered sugar, fluffy marshmallows are known to perfectly suit campfires, sweet potatoes, and hot cocoa. Marshmallow candy dates back to ancient Egypt and was flavored with the extract from the root of the marsh mallow plant, *Althaea officinalis*. Reserved for special celebrations, the candy was actually honey-flavored with the extract of the root. The thick syrup was also used as a medicinal ointment.

European confectioners in the 1850s whipped and sweetened the root sap with sugar, creating a fluffy, aerated piece of candy. Soon, quicker ways to produce the popular candy were found and gelatin and starch replaced actual mallow root as the primary ingredients.

Now marshmallows are molded and extruded into various shapes and flavors. Banana-flavored circus peanuts and Peeps are both made of marshmallow.

CHEWING GUM

Photo Tamara Staples
Collection Jeff Nelson

A sweetened substance made specifically for chewing. The main ingredient is usually a substance called chicle. Our ancient ancestors were the original inventors of gum chewing, on saps and resins mixed with beeswax. Ancient Greeks enjoyed chomping mastiche from the mastic tree, and this sap-based gum can still be found today.

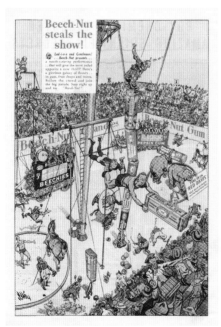

Mayans chewed chicle sap from the sapodilla tree. Chicle is an important ingredient in gum today. It was introduced to Thomas Adams by the former Mexican president and general, Antonio Lopez de Santa Anna.

Unable to manufacture rubber from the sap, Adams boiled a small batch of chicle in his kitchen to create a chewing gum. He gave some to a local store to sell and before long was selling his licorice-flavored Black Jack Gum everywhere.

Soon, many manufacturers were making gum. Wrigley started as a soap salesman, giving away gum made by the Zeno Manufacturing Company as a bonus for purchasing his product. Beeman's pepsin chewing gum relieved indigestion. The Frank H. Fleer Company sold Chiclets by the ounce and later invented bubble gum. Dentyne was developed as a "dental gum." Today, gum comes in a rainbow of flavors, shapes, packages, and sizes, with sugar and without.

BUBBLE GUM

Frank Fleer, maker of Chiclets, invented Blibber-Blubber in 1906 but the inferior sticky mess never hit the shelves. Years later, in 1928, Walter Diemer, while working for the Frank H. Fleer Gum Company, devised a successful formula. Diemer, an accountant for Fleer, was experimenting with a rubber formula and by blunder discovered bubble gum. The first batch was pink because that was the only color on-hand that day at the Fleer Company. Most bubble gum has been pink since. Dubble Bubble became a hit after test marketing in Philadelphia in December 1928. Bazooka, Bubble Yum, and Dubble Bubble are archetypical bubble gums.

The sticky pink elastic may have been banned in Singapore, but it has been proven to relieve stress, calm nerves, aid concentration, and bring happiness to millions of gum chewers and bubble blowers around the world.

Photos by Tamara Staples
From the gum collection of Jeff Nelson

HARD CANDY

Hard candies are a simple candy concoction of heated sugar and water. We call it hard candy because a large percent of moisture is extracted by heat. Sour balls, peppermints, lozenges, or drops all originally had medicinal purposes. Shapes vary; they can be shaped like discs, ribbon, canes, and sticks. They can have a filling center or a flavor added to the sugar. Lollipops and suckers are essentially hard candy on a stick. Originally, lollipops were hard candy stuck on the end of a slate pencil and were intended for children to help them stay clean and to prevent choking.

CHOCOLATE

Deliciously Good

Chocolates are sweets that have a chocolate filling or ingredients that are mixed with chocolate. *Theobroma cacao*, chocolate's scientific name, means "food of the gods" as it was used in Mayan and Aztec ceremonies. This beautiful substance can take on many delicious forms. It begins with the tropical cocoa bean that is extracted from the pod of the cacao tree. The beans are first fermented and dried. Then the beans are shelled and their insides or nibs ground into a paste called chocolate liquor. The extracted cocoa butter, the natural fat, becomes a separate substance. The chocolate is refined further, and, depending on its destiny, various ingredients are added.

Chocolate can be formed into unsweetened milk or dark chocolate depending on the ratio of cocoa butter to chocolate liquor. Chocolate is sold in powdered, liquid, and solid states. It can be the creamy center of a candy or drizzled on the outside. It can be molded into bars and other shapes and extruded in a liquid form. Today, with its infinite possibilities and vast popularity, chocolate's given scientific name still stands.

FUDGE

A cross between a creamy fondant and a caramel, semi-soft fudge is made by cooking sugar along with other ingredients until the sugar has almost crystallized. Popular flavors include chocolate and maple and often include nuts. The first fudge, according to candy lore, was a batch of caramels gone wrong. The candy makers apparently tasted the finely crystallized concoction and cried, "Oh, fudge."

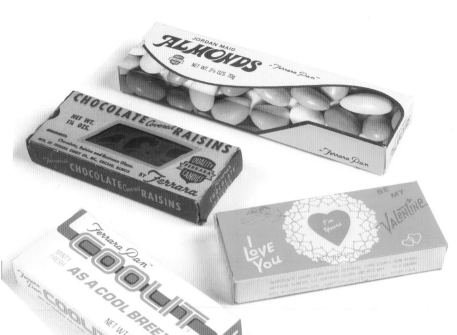

PANNED CANDY

A panned candy is a small confection with a distinct center and a coating. Nuts, malted milk balls, raisins, or small hard candies can all be panned and coated with chocolate or a colored shell. This process of mixing a center in a pan, thereby creating a casing, is one of the oldest industrial methods of making candy. First invented in 17th century France to make dragees, the panning process, while done primarily by machine today, has remained essentially the same for the last 300 years. The French mixed nuts and spices in a bowl filled with sugar and syrup until the nuts were coated with a candy shell. Today, large rotating copper or stainless pans do the heavy work, while master confectioners apply their true art in adding the ingredients and adjusting the temperature to create a perfect shell. Coated candy centers can be polished in a pan to give them a shine. Chocolate-covered raisins, Boston baked beans, and jawbreakers are examples of panned candies.

CHAPTER 4

Marathon Candy Bar

Introduced by M&M Mars in 1974, the Marathon bar was a delicious eight inches of perfectly braided caramel covered in milk chocolate. We know the exact length, thanks to the yellow ruler printed on the back of the bold, red wrapper. The bar was a favorite for its somewhat simple taste. I remember the way the caramel would string out of control, sending chocolate bits airborne, all with one delicious bite. As the lengthy candy bar really did seemingly run on forever, the name Marathon was appropriate.

A successful cartoon advertising campaign, Marathon Mike and the Pirates, was discontinued in the late 1970s, and subsequently, Marathon sales slumped. M&M Mars took the candy off the shelves for good in 1981, aborting the Marathon run after only a short sprint.

In 1990, to insure the candy legend was completely over, the company changed the name of their U.K. Marathon bar. Britain's Marathon was not formulated like the U.S. version; it was comprised of chocolate, caramel, and peanut. The last British Marathon bars were renamed Snickers after their popular U.S. counterparts.

There is a European bar called Curly Wurly, made by Cadbury in England, that some say is a close caramel cousin. To others, it will never touch the braided beauty of the Marathon bar.

Dan Goodsell Collection

Bonomo's Turkish Taffy

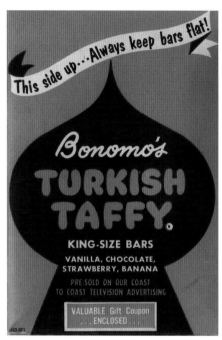

Michael Rosenberg Collection

Sources say Bonomo's Turkish Taffy was a wonderful slab of chewy candy — a real long-lasting delight. Victor Bonomo's Turkish father was a Coney Island candy maker, specializing in saltwater taffy and hard candies. After World War II, the family briefly made candy bars but came back exclusively to taffy when their lovely Bonomo's Turkish Taffy took off.

The famous chewy vanilla taffy recipe came from candy cooks simply exploring in the Bonomo's Coney Island candy kitchen. It is neither a family recipe nor real taffy — it was actually a type of nougat.

Originally, the candy was distributed in pans and broken up for sale at the local candy counter. When the candy bits became popular, the company then packaged the taffy into long pieces and added flavors like strawberry, chocolate, and banana. The bars were packaged in wax wrappers and included an image of several men in fezzes, happily making candy.

In the 1950s, Bonomo's Turkish Taffy ran a popular ad campaign on children's TV programs featuring three puppets named Bo, No, and Mo. At the height of the Bonomo's Turkish Taffy reign, the company was employing hundreds at their plant and making close to 100 million taffy bars a year.

After Victor, the second-generation Bonomo, retired in 1970, the company changed owners a few times and in 1980 became part of Tootsie Roll Industries. Sadly, due to lack of sales and true taffy lovers, the candy was discontinued in 1980. No-Mo'-Bo's Turkish Taffy.

A candy produced today called Dosher's French Chew is truly a brethren to the Bonomo piece. Just close your eyes, recall the men in fezzes, and chew.

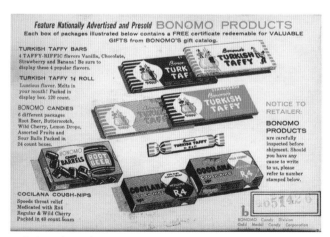

Michael Rosenberg Collection

Seven Up Bar

Remember the heavenly Seven Up bar? The tagline on the candy wrapper read, "Small Taste of Candy in a Bar." The St. Paul-based Pearson's Candy Company, makers of Nut Goodie, Bun Bar, and Salted Nut Roll, also made the Seven Up. In 1951, Pearson's purchased the Trudeau Candy Company, known for the famed Seven Up bar, and continued to make the candy until the late 1970s.

The bar comprised multiple pieces covered in dark chocolate, and for a short time. milk chocolate. The Seven Up candy bar had seven small individual pillows, each filled with their own delicious centers. The fillings changed at various times but started with several types of caramel, Brazil nut, coconut, and jelly. The yummy collective candy bar was discontinued in 1979. At that time, the seven pockets were filled with coconut, mint cream, nougat, butterscotch, fudge, buttercream, and caramel centers.

The bar really was a treat for those of us who were indecisive about our candy — we could have it all in one candy bar. It was like going to the ice cream store and tasting seven flavors. The Seven Up bar was better than Napoleon cake. It was complete with all the crowd-pleasing favorites, right there, in one bar.

Sources at Pearson's say that the bar was discontinued because the name, shared for a while with a large soda manufacturer, had trademark rights that expired. In addition, it was an expensive little bar to make; all those separate fillings were costly and the labor involved to inject the pockets was high.

The Seven Up bar does have a close relative that is still made today. It is NECCO's Skybar with four fillings — caramel, vanilla, peanut, and fudge. Although the number of centers is less, the NECCO classic is a tasty treat for those who still want it all.

Dan Goodsell Collection

Trudeau's **SevenUp**
7 Delicious Varieties in One Bar

5¢

TWENTY FOUR 5¢ BARS

The only bar of its kind in America. An assortment of dollar per pound chocolates in a 5c bar. A favorite with the consumer for over a quarter of a century.

Delicious Creamy Caramel
Double Vanilla Creams
Maple Walnut Creams
Brazil Nut Caramel
Apple Butter Pectin Jelly
Chocolate Pudding
Coconut Cream

TRUDEAU CANDIES, INC., ST. PAUL, MINN.

Michael Rosenberg Collection

Wacky Packages

Wacky Packages were vile parody trading cards that ridiculed companies and their top-brand products from 1967 to 1992. *New York Magazine* ran an article in 1973 calling Topps Wacky Packages revolutionary and featuring sticker graphics on the cover. In the wacky world lived the angry Jolly Mean Giant, crunching distraught pea heads. Chock Full of Nuts and Bolts was a very unsavory looking coffee. Kook Aid was a tropical drink pitcher gone off. Playbug Magazine was entertainment for insects featuring a foxy aphid head babe on a beach.

Wacky Packages created a collecting frenzy among kids, as they were distinctly different from sports cards. They were appealing to both boys and girls, satirically smart and simply put — they were cool. Kids cherished the cards that mocked the products they knew because of the corny TV ads that interrupted their favorite shows. Wacky Packages potty trained a generation to appreciate *Saturday Night Live*, *National Lampoon*, and *Spy Magazine*.

No commercial product was spared, and even Topps own products got a good roasting. The cards featured the added bonus of a sticky back, which allowed collections to be displayed on Mead folders, bedroom windows, lockers, and skateboards. They were rarely bound up in rubber bands and kept in shoeboxes under beds. They were portable *Mad Magazine* spreads.

The cards were huge sellers in the 1970s, and, because so many were actually stuck, they have become very rare. Collectors today dedicate websites and magazines to the stickers, paying homage to illustrators Norm Saunders and Art Spiegelman, both of whom produced art for the cards.

After a few cease-and-desist orders, along with the threat of a group lawsuit by major companies who didn't want their brands tarnished for future consumers, the cards fizzled out in the early 1990s. One 1991 card, Prez Broccoli dispenser, depicts a George Bush, Sr., head on a Pez dispenser spewing out heads of broccoli. It's fun to imagine what they'd do to George W. if they were still making those fine parody cards today.

Slaytex LIVING GLOVES

FITS NECKS PERFECTLY

 * © 1979 TOPPS CHEWING GUM, INC. PRTD. IN U.S.A.

RAW GOO

MAKES YOUR STOMACH ROAR!

UN COOKED SPAGHETTI SAUCE

 * © 1979 TOPPS CHEWING GUM, INC. PRTD. IN U.S.A.

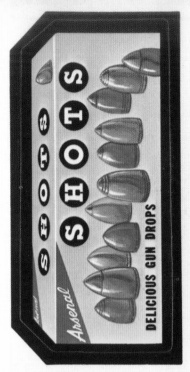

SHOTS

Arsenal

DELICIOUS GUN DROPS

* © 1979 TOPPS CHEWING GUM, INC. PRTD. IN U.S.A.

SHOT WHEELS
CHEAPEST HEAPS IN THE WORLD

A MUDDLED TOY

13

OW!

GUARANTEED TO SELF DESTRUCT

 * © 1979 TOPPS CHEWING GUM, INC. PRTD. IN U.S.A.

PIWI

JUNGLE SHOE POLISH

FOR MUDDY PYGMIES

BLECCH

1 ounce NIT-WIT

BLECCH PIWI BLECCH

* © 1979 TOPPS CHEWING GUM, INC. PRTD. IN U.S.A.

HaHa CRACKERS

Funshine

THEY'LL CRACK YOU UP!

MADE ON THE FUNNY FARM

HaHa CRACKERS

3 CHUCKLES IN EVERY PACKAGE

NET WT. 10 YUKS

 * © 1979 TOPPS CHEWING GUM, INC. PRTD. IN U.S.A.

COVER IT!

TRAC

GANGSTERS

* © 1979 TOPPS CHEWING GUM, INC. PRTD. IN U.S.A.

Peter Pain

Peter Pain

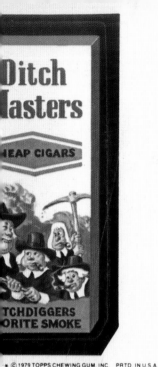

Ditch Masters
CHEAP CIGARS
TCHDIGGERS
ORITE SMOKE
© 1979 TOPPS CHEWING GUM, INC. PRTD. IN U.S.A

SMITH SISTERS
Weird Chicks
SMITH SISTERS
FEMININE COUGH DROPS
© 1979 TOPPS CHEWING GUM, INC. PRTD. IN U.S.A

Head &
Boulders
shampoo
FLIP YOUR WIG WITH
FOR PEOPLE WITH ROCKS IN THEIR HEADS!
© 1979 TOPPS CHEWING GUM, INC. PRTD. IN U.S.A

ticks
WO
PAC
WITH 1 STICK
STINKY
BUBBLE GUM

© 1979

edi-Quak
LIEF FOR DUCKS
's for the birds
SOOTHING RELIEF FOR SHOTGUN WOUNDS, OVEN BURNS AND FEATHER PLUCKING
© 1979 TOPPS CHEWING GUM, INC. PRTD. IN U.S.A

Sunstroke
Creature Crackers
THE SNACK THAT ATTACKS!
NEW CONVENIENT RECLOSABLE TOP
Sunstroke Creature Crackers
6¢

$500 A PIECE
THE EXPENSIVE CANDY THAT TAKES A BITE-O-MONEY
BIT-O-MONEY
BIT-O-MONEY

LISTERIN
BLIST
MONSTER
FRIES GERM
Bad breath than no b
BLISTERINE

SOFT-HEAD
BULBS
GD
SOFT-HEAD
BULBS
GE

GOONMAN'S
GOONMAN'S

Fee
FLAVOR WITH A
Fee
10 toes in

Blackjack Gum

The deliciously spicy Blackjack Gum was one of the first commercially-produced gums. Thomas Adams, who had experimented successfully with chicle, the main ingredient in gum, conceived it. Adam was one of the forefathers of chewing gum.

In 1871, after much success with his first gum, Adams No. 1, he began to add flavors to his products. He experimented with natural flavorings — like sarsaparilla — without much luck. Flavorings had to be strong enough to last but not too overpowering.

In 1884, he tested a gum with a licorice flavor and called his invention Adams' Blackjack. It was the first flavored gum in America and the first gum to be offered in a stick form. Before that, chewing gum was sold in an uneven lump or chunk. Adams predicted that by making gum more uniform and flavorful, it would appeal to more customers. The licorice-based Blackjack Gum, priced at one penny for two sticks, would go on to delight gum chewers for years.

Adams continued to have success with chewing gum. His Tutti-Frutti chewing gum was the first to be sold in vending machines. These machines, which Adams designed, first appeared 1888 at train station platforms in New York. Adams is also credited with crafting the first gumball machines. During Prohibition, Adam advertised the breath-freshening benefits of his tasty gums directly to drinkers.

Blackjack sold well into the 1970s. But with the introduction of fabulous new flavors, packaging, and sugarless gums, Blackjack production was halted because of slow sales. New flavors of Freshen-Up, Trident, and Bubble Yum were packaged in hi-tech foil wrappers with updated logos. The younger gum set appeared in ads and commercials. The straightforward Blackjack started seeming like an old-timer gum and couldn't keep up with the modern whippersnapper novelties on the market.

Adams Gum Company purchased American Chicle Company. Then Warner-Lambert Company, now part of Pfizer Pharmaceuticals, ultimately purchased the company.

Every so often, Warner-Lambert will manufacture a run of Blackjack and other old-time favorites Beeman's and Clove because of customer requests. Currently, Blackjack licorice gum, the original flavored gum, is unavailable.

Jeff Nelson Collection

Michael Rosenberg Collection

Chicken Dinner

A tribute must be paid to Chicken Dinner candy bar because it was a top-selling, well-loved bar, despite the fact that it had an outrageous name and contained no chicken. I am too young to have known this candy myself, but devotees swear that this was the best candy bar in history. The salty-sweet chocolate peanut roll has a cult following like no other. Collectors clamor for old wrappers and other nostalgic items. Chicken Dinner enthusiasts wax on tirelessly about the candy on web pages.

The reason for the commotion may be that the candy was never produced by a big company and was always fresh. Among the bigger mass-produced bars, it felt special and tasted handmade. It was developed at a time when candy was seen as a necessary and healthy food, not an indulgent treat. The Chicken Dinner name implied the bar was like a satisfying meal, fresh from the oven. An entire roasted chicken was depicted on early wrappers, denoting a hearty meal.

Sperry Candy Company in Milwaukee, Wisconsin, produced this historic piece, along with some other crazy-sounding chocolate bars like Denver Sandwich and Cold Turkey.

Pearson's Candy in Minneapolis bought the Sperry Company in 1962. Pearson's, makers of many classic candies themselves, decided to fry the Chicken Dinner, so to speak. The candy bar melted into history.

CANDY

Chicken

SPERRY
CANDY CO.
MILWAUKEE, WIS.

Dinner

5¢

NET WT. 2-1/2 OZ.

A SPERRY candy

Chicken   Dinner

Contains: Sugar, Corn Syrup, Condensed Whole Milk, Condensed Skimmed Milk, Peanuts, Cocoa Butter, Cocoanut Oil Stearine, Dried Egg-White, Tartaric Acid, Salt, Vanilla, Lecithin, Artificially Flavored with Vanillin, Sweet Milk Chocolate.

Beth Kimmerle Collection

POWER HOUSE

IS AMERICA'S BEST CANDY VALUE. ITS PLEASING COMBINATION OF CARAMEL, FUDGE AND CRISP NUTS GENEROUSLY COVERED WITH RICH CHOCOLATE EXCELS ALL OTHERS IN QUALITY AND GOODNESS.

POWER
HOUSE

TRADE MARK REG., U.S. PAT. OFF.

POWER HOUSE

5¢

POWER
HOUSE

NET WEIGHT 2-3/4 OZS.

5¢ MFD. BY WALTER H. JOHNSON CANDY CO., CHICAGO, ILL.

POWER HOUSE

IS MANUFACTURED WITH THE FOLLOWING WHOLESOME INGREDIENTS SUGAR CORN

Beth Kimmerle Collection

Powerhouse Bar

There is something tragic about anything that was once a powerhouse but is no longer. A candy bar is no exception. It was called a Powerhouse because it was a hefty bad boy, 4 ounces of caramel, peanuts, and fudge. Most candy bars are less than 2 ounces today.

The Walter Johnson Candy Company originally produced the bar sometime in the 1920s when candy bar sales were booming. By the 1940s, the popular bar was sponsoring comics in the Sunday newspaper. Their cartoon character, Roger Wilco, offered kids fantastic prizes for 15 cents and a Powerhouse wrapper. Roger Wilco's sci-fi treats, like Magni-Ray rings and secret decoders, were low-tech space age toys kids readily saved their allowance and wrappers for. The adventuresome Roger Wilco got his name from the classic sign-off at the end of a radio transmission.

Roger Wilco, as strapping as the bar he was promoting, reminded children, "Candy is delicious food — especially if it is a Powerhouse candy bar — enjoy some everyday! Powerhouse remains your biggest and most delicious nickel's worth." Many now remember sharing the oversized bar amongst a few friends or saving the thing for weeks, nibbling off bits at a time.

Walter Johnson Candy became part of Peter Paul Candy in the late 1960s, and Powerhouse joined other popular candy bars like Almond Joy and Mounds. But things changed, and the massive Powerhouse got slenderized and less significant. The 4 ounces of pure candy power dwindled to a measly 2, and the bar stopped living up to its name. It was finally discontinued forever when Peter Paul was sold to Hershey in 1988.

We'll bid adieu to the once full-on Powerhouse candy bar with an ending it deserves: "Roger, Powerhouse, over and out."

Beth Kimmerle Collection

THE INTERIOR OF A CANDY FACTORY

CHAPTER 5

At any given time, large vats of ingredients whoosh by, circulating both delicate and forceful aromatic smells. The sounds of nearby copper kettles ring like primitive instruments, while combining sweet candy with colored coatings. Various flavors and ingredients dot the air with a spectacle like the Fourth of July. Candy churns back and forth from liquid to solid and hot to cold, aided along by workers specially trained in their fine craft.

Typical candy factories are large-scale candy-making environments with separate rooms for making a range of candy and processing their various ingredients. Most factories feature hot and cold extremes. Coolers are kept at well below freezing, while candy can be cooked to hundreds of degrees. Productions are in buildings, spreading over sevaral city blocks or sometimes covering miles. Often ingredients are shipped to a factory in bulk — chocolate blocks, 50-pound bags of peanuts, truckloads of corn syrup, and massive amounts of sugar.

Most factories, for safety and security reasons, are closed off to the candy-adoring public. In addition, factories are ever concerned with trade secrets, custom machinery, and special recipes. Receiving an invitation to visit a candy factory is a unique honor.

Factories are inner-sugar sanctums, glorious processing centers where fresh ingredients are miraculously turned into delicious candy.

I have been lucky to visit many factories and on occasion have brought a photographer to help capture the experience. Tamara Staples has been shooting wonderful portraits, still lifes, and interiors for years and was the perfect accompanist to the inner sanctum of a factory. She appreciates a candy fresh from the conveyer belt and has a keen eye. Together we won the proverbial golden ticket; Tamara took pictures while I chatted with candy-making experts. We ate much candy, met the workers, and shared our experience here.

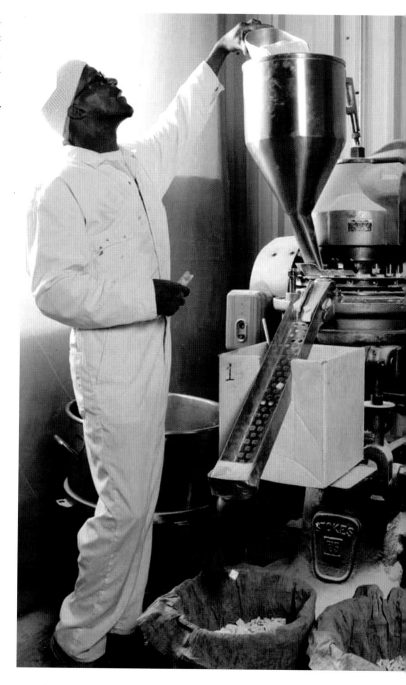

Derrick, master confectioner at C. Howard's, scoops violet-flavored sugar powder into a machine that will press the mixture into scented squares.

(Opposite) Grade A peanuts, fresh from a roaster, are checked for quality by Janet Cody (left) and Denise Biel. Janet has spent 24 years and Denise 30 years working with candy at Goldenberg's Peanut Chew factory.
Photos Tamara Staples

Debra has been an enrobing room assistant at Goldenberg's for almost 25 years.
Photo Tamara Staples

Goetze Candy workers put the cream in a caramel. From left to right, Patricia Maccord, Margaret Telakowicz, Spaulding Goetze, Sr., Frank Rynarzewski, Vernon T. Hart, Jr., Jane Kent, Linda Garrett, and Mitchell Goetze.

(Opposite) Debra Cassel helps Goldenberg's Peanut Chews into a chocolate bath. Debra has been an enrobing room assistant at Goldenberg's for almost 25 years.

Photos Tamara Staples

Annabelle Candy Company

Sam Altshuler, a Russian immigrant who arrived in the United States in 1917, started his Annabelle Candy Company in 1950. He taught himself the art of candy making while fiddling around on the stove as a fruit purveyor. After years of perfecting his technique, Sam hit the jackpot with a delectable candy bar. It combined marshmallow, cashews, malt, and chocolate. With a delicious candy, Sam went into the candy business full time. He named his new candy endeavor, the Annabelle Candy Company, after his daughter and officially began manufacturing the right-on Rocky Road in San Francisco.

Rocky Road quickly gained popularity throughout the western United States and remains a top-selling West Coast favorite. In 1965, Annabelle Candy Company moved across the San Francisco Bay to its present location in Hayward, California.

Sam Altshuler, self-taught candy maker, passed away in 1971, leaving control of the thriving candy company to his daughter, the company namesake, Annabelle Altshuler Block. Shortly after Sam's death, Annabelle Candy purchased two companies: the Golden Nugget Candy Company, of San Francisco, the makers of Big Hunk and Look candy bars; and the Cardinet Candy Co., which manufactured U-NO and Abba-Zaba candy bars. All of these classic favorites, in addition to the original Rocky Road, continue to roll along in production in Hayward today. Unlike the title of their original candy bar, the thoroughfare for Annabelle Candy has been exceedingly sound.

The Annabelle Candy Company grew as Annabelle's son, Gary Gogol, managed its business operations for many years. Annabelle's daughter, Susan Gamson Karl, currently manages the company as president and CEO. Susan, granddaughter of Sam, effectively grew up at the candy factory. She has many fond candy memories of thrilling factory tours and still remembers the delicious sight of chocolate swirling in huge vats. Sometimes she would return home from a day at the factory, covered from head to toe in chocolate. Having grown up with them, she sees her many employees as family members. Some dedicated Annabelle workers have been with the company for over 30 years.

(Above) Abba-Zaba was recently featured as an excellent munchie in the movie, *Half Baked*.

(Left) Rocky Road, Annabelle's marshmallow treat

What started as a family business continues today as the one of the largest independently owned candy-bar manufacturers in the United States, producing some of the most popular and traditional West Coast candies. With packaging and flavors only slightly updated from the originals, the Annabelle candies are nostalgic favorites. Currently, in the fight against the homogeneous candy world, the Annabelle Candy Company manufactures a total of eight different candy bars, all icons of many a childhood, including Rocky Road, Big Hunk, U-NO, Look!, and last but not least Abba-Zaba peanut butter taffy.

U-NO – pronounced "you know" – is another California classic.

Rocky Road candy advertised at a California fairground in the 1950s.

ALSO *Try*

LOOK

chocolate nut chew

BIG HUNK

Delicious CHEWY NOUGA[T]

with NUTS

Big Hunk display box 1960s.

GOLDEN NUGGET CANDY COMPANY

Atkinson Candy Company

Atkinson Candy Company has carried on the family tradition of making and selling candy since 1932. B.E. Atkinson and his wife, Mabel, started the company. Located in Texas, the firm is known for its fine quality candy, including some of the best peanut butter and peppermint hard candies available. "Naturally, we're Texas proud," says President Eric Atkinson, "but our candy is sold all over the world."

The company today comprises two separate manufacturing facilities, both in Texas, each specializing in making different candy. Atkinson Candy bought the neighboring Judson Candy Company in 1983, and between them they produce everything from jelly beans to fruit slices and marshmallow pieces to mints. This company is famous for their Chick-O-Stick candy piece, a crunchy peanut butter and toasted coconut candy stick. Some compare the golden wonder to the inside of a Butterfinger. If you have yet to taste one, imagine fresh-roasted Texas Grade A Jumbo peanuts sprinkled, while they're still warm, with salt and ground along with pure granulated sugar in a process so superior it is patented. Candy makers take the concoction and form it into sticks that are a mix of peanuts and the crunchy candy. Then each Chick-O-Stick is dusted with freshly toasted coconut. It's flaky and crunchy, crispy yet chewy, very peanutty, and really quite delicious.

Why is it called a Chick-O-Stick? The Atkinsons say their grandfather came up with the name one day, and, well, it just stuck. Everyone knows, however, that the stick looks more than a bit like a slender chicken leg. Was an extra large Texas chicken his inspiration? Whatever the truth about the name origin is, we can all testify that this piece, so unique and delicious, is a nostalgic classic. The third generation of the Atkinson family now runs the business, making over 64 million pieces of Chick-O-Stick candy each year. The brother and sister team, Eric and Amy Atkinson, share the daily work with their father who is still very involved in the candy business.

Vintage 1960s packaging
Michael Rosenberg Collection

The Atkinson candy plant in the 1940s.

Atkinson candy plant.

Ben Myerson Candy Company

Ben Myerson began working in the candy industry for a company called E.A. Hoffman Candies in 1912. Hoffman Candies made popular candy bars like the Habit Bar and Chicken Bone. They also produced boxed chocolates that included pictures of famous Hollywood starlets. The candy boxes, featuring black-and-white headshots of actresses, became highly collectible — and still are today. Starting as a salesperson, Ben learned all about the delicious business of sweets and quickly became a partner. Successful with candy, he went on to form his very own Ben Myerson Candy Company, in Los Angeles, in 1937.

He invented the popular Good News bar shortly after starting his company. The handmade Good News bar is currently the most popular candy bar sold in Hawaii. However, that is one of the only places it is still found. When production costs increased, the company attempted to discontinue the bar. The loyal candy lovers in Hawaii would not hear of it. The bar is now legendary and anyone on a trip to the Islands will surely notice it everywhere. This tropical favorite was formed after Bob Myerson had a son and wanted to spread the "Good News" about the arrival of his baby. Early wrappers looked like the front page of a newspaper.

Ben Myerson's sons, Bob and Jim, joined the business in the 1940s. At that time, they were producing a full line of assorted chocolates and chocolate bars with entertaining names like the Alice Holiday Bar and Cherry Thyme, the forerunner to their now classic Big Cherry. To this day, they continue to produce the traditional Big Cherry, a throwback fondant candy that is simply heavenly. This cherry and chocolate combination, wrapped in a candy-pink wrapper, is top rate.

Big Cherry, the cherry fondant dream from Ben Myerson Candy.

The Ben Myerson Candy Company's own good news and success continued as business developed. Located in Los Angeles, the company grew along with the film industry. Having a manufacturing facility close to the exciting Hollywood scene was advantageous. Movie stars always needed candy. The factory was even featured in pictures — it was rented out for a *Ma and Pa Kettle* movie.

In 1955, the thriving company acquired Christopher's Candy, the oldest candy company in Southern California. Christopher's had manufactured chocolate products since 1887. In 1932, they started producing a pure fruit-pectin jelly candy dusted with fine sugar for the Sunkist Growers Cooperative. The delicious candy was like biting into a piece of fresh-grown, sun-sweetened California fruit. The candy quickly became the company's best-selling piece. In 1974, the great relationship with the fruit growers led to a license arrangement to use the Sunkist name on a candy line — and Sunkist Fruit Gems were born.

The good news continues. Bob's son, Jim Myerson, the one that the Good News candy bar was developed for, represents the third generation of Myersons in the candy industry. The company now produces over 2,000,000 of their Sunkist Fruit Gems every day along with the classic Big Cherry and regional darling Good News candy bar.

Easter Greetings

Christopher's

Christopher's candy card circa 1900.

Christopher's was purchased by Ben Myerson in 1955. Currently the company produces everything from Sunkist Fruit Gems to the limited-edition Good News candy bar.

Boyer Candy Company

The Mallo Cup, Smoothie, and Peanut Butter Cups, made by the Boyer Candy Company in Altoona, Pennsylvania, are produced today right where they started. Two young brothers, William and Bob Boyer, founded the candy company in the early 1930s. They started the business primarily to bring in extra income during the lean Depression years. Early on, Bob sold their homemade fudge and nut raisin rolls door-to-door, while William and their mother, Emily, produced and wrapped the candy.

The family soon began to distribute their candy products to local amusement parks. These carnival distractions were gaining popularity during the Depression, as they were welcome escapes from the realities of life. The American public was enjoying the rides and shows along with a piece of candy or two. When Emily Boyer's kitchen became overrun with candy supplies and sugar bags, the family moved their thriving operation to a nearby factory. There they expanded their line to include hand-decorated, chocolate-molded animals and eventually the much-loved Mallo Cup.

Boyer's Bite Size Candy Cup Box circa 1950s.

The Mallo Cup originally started as a chocolate-covered marshmallow bar. However, problems with the sensitive marshmallow inspired the inventive Mrs. Boyer to pour marshmallow into a chocolate-lined cup used for cupcakes. The candy went from Mallo Bar to Mallo Cup and became a huge hit that was much easier to make. With the success of the new cup and the brothers' partnership officially incorporated, what was once a little family-run outfit began to blossom.

In the 1940s, the company introduced a coupon that kids could save for prizes and candy. Boyer Gold Coin cards were redeemable for treats like tea sets, jewelry, and art supplies. Still in use today, the early marketing plan was a huge success. Soon, both the Smoothie Cup and the Peanut Butter Cup were part of the offerings, and the company moved away from other candy and concentrated on its top sellers, delicious candy centers served up in a chocolate cup.

As the company grew, offers to purchase Boyer came from many neighboring candy companies. After 40 years of making candy, the Boyer family sold their business in 1969. A confection supplier called American Maize Products, a corn syrup manufacturer, became the lucky bidder. American Maize attempted to grow the company through new items like the Minty Mallo, Bunch O'Nuts, Jamboree, and Fluffernutter. With only small successes, American Maize, in turn, sold Boyer to the expert Forgione family in 1984.

The Forgiones' company, Consolidated Brands, was well-seasoned in the food industry. They had enjoyed a long and successful history in ice creams, syrups, and chocolates. Anthony Forgione took what he learned from his other companies and expanded Boyer Candy Company to include toppings, sauces, and foiled and molded chocolates. He eventually had a successful business that was centered around the very famous and delicious candy cups.

Lakemont Park was founded in 1894 and was one of the first amusement park accounts of the Boyer brothers. When the candy company had a picnic there, one of the employees suggested building Boyertown USA, a candy tribute park. Anthony, paying homage to the company's amusement park roots, developed the candy amusement park. He even bought some old roller coasters and had them shipped to the Boyertown location. Boyertown USA was later sold but remains a park, where you can still find the delicious and famous Boyer Mallo Cup.

Boyer Mallo Cup Matches.

Boyer's Mallow Cup display Boxes.

C. Howards' 10-cent display sign from the 1950s.

C. Howard

In 1934, an Armenian immigrant had an idea for a violet-flavored mint tablet. The unique flavoring was common in Europe but hard to find in America. Floral-flavored candies have been popular since the Middle Ages when sugar was used to candy flowers like violets and miniature roses. Upon arriving in the United States, the man changed his name to Charles Howard and named his company after his new American-style moniker. The candy itself is still called Choward's Violet Mints, while the company is referred to as C. Howard.

Early on, Charles Howard sold his Choward's Violet mint tablets door-to-door from small trays. As his business grew, he hired packers to hand pack the tablets into small foil covered rolls. In the beginning of his candy career, C. Howard had a location on lower Broadway in New York in what is now known as SoHo. Smelling the strong mysterious scent of violet, customers would knock on the door to ask for samples.

In the late 1930s, Elizabeth Juhase, an especially good employee, helped Charles grow his business by managing his sales office as well as the other employers, some of whom were her sisters. Soon, the growing company was located in a large loft building on Fifth Avenue. When C. Howard, the entrepreneurial immigrant, died in 1969, he had no family members. He left his candy company to his devoted employee, Elizabeth, who at the time was 60 years old.

In time, the unusual candy caught on, and the company developed other flavors. The firm started to manufacture its own candy in the early 1960s and eventually moved its candy act to Long Island. In the early 1970s, Elizabeth hired her nephew Kenneth to help with operations. Kenneth, fresh from a stint in the Army, came to the candy business with an understanding of mechanics and worked with the complicated candy equipment.

C. Howard's distinctive violet mints and gum have changed little over the years.

In 1985, Elizabeth passed away after almost 50 years in the candy business. She left her victorious violet candy operation to her three nephews, Kenneth, Arthur, and Gene Pratz, all of whom are still involved in the business today. In the name of tradition, Michael Pratz, Arthur's son, is currently working at the factory.

Also working at C. Howards are a handful of other people, who mix flavors, make boxes, and wrap candies. Those that are not family are like family. You won't find Chowards candy in just any store. The small line features the mysterious and elusive mints in violet, lemon, spearmint, and peppermint. They also make a wonderfully singular Choward's violet scented tablet gum. Those who carry it know that the unusual flavors don't appeal to just any palate. Only refined consumers appreciate the taste. Others use it as an air freshener.

These candies are the epitome of nostalgic. Their charming foil packaging changes because of new FDA requirements and not because of new marketing schemes. The company does not sell to the mass-market chains because, as Kenneth put it, "I work too hard to give my candy away." And indeed they all do. The brothers Pratz do it all — rebuild equipment, handle sales, pack orders, go to candy shows, and answer phones. Visiting the factory, I met people that for the love of candy continue do it the old-fashioned way.

Not just for wise guys, Smarties classic candy discs have changed little since the 1950s.

Ce De Candy

Edward Dee, who came to the United States from Britain in 1949, started Ce De Candy. Edward brought with him candy experience he had gained from working with popular confection producers overseas. His training at the European candy company Swizzles-Matlow guided him to his quick success in the American candy business.

He started his small-time operation in a rented New Jersey garage. He began with a wrapping machine, a small disc presser, and fruit-flavored sugar ingredients. His first creation was a candy he called Smarties. He took the name from a popular United Kingdom chocolate candy that was similar to M&Ms. The company, Rowntree and Macintosh, which produced the chocolate cousin, had not trademarked the name in the United States, allowing Dee use of the catchy candy title.

Dee grew his business from garage to factory, and by 1972 the company had several manufacturing sites producing the pastel candy pellets. Ce De's yummy Smarties, initially a Halloween staple, had become an everyday favorite and were sold at stores across the country.

Ce De continues to make its classic cello-wrapped Smarties in flavors that have not changed much since the 1950s. The most popular color, white, is an orange-cream flavor. Over the years, the company has added candy necklaces, plastic-molded, sugar-filled fruit shapes, along with lollipops and lipsticks to their line-up.

In 1991, the company sought a character who could help promote their candy and landed a deal with the infamous Mr. T. The mohawked spokesman helped propel the company, sell a lot of candy, and raise thousands of dollars for the Children's Defense Fund charity. Their collaboration called Crusade for Kids encouraged children to stay in school and eat candy instead of using drugs. Mr. T, wearing Ce De candy jewelry instead of his flashy gold, pitied the fool who did not indulge in the colorful candy.

Today, Smarties can also be found in tropical and super-sour flavors and are pressed into various shapes and sizes. The candy regularly tops the charts as a favorite nonchocolate candy item. Ce De remains family-owned and operated. Edward Dee's son, Jonathan, now oversees the business, helping the company produce over two billion rolls of their sweet signature candy every year.

No. 404
JET PLASTIC PLANES
—24 Count Display Box
Packed: 36 Boxes Per Case

No. 401
POPEYE CANDY CIGARETTES
—24 Count Display Box
Packed: 24 Boxes Per Case

No. 400
CANDY NECKLACES
—48 Count Display Box
Packed: 12 Boxes Per Case

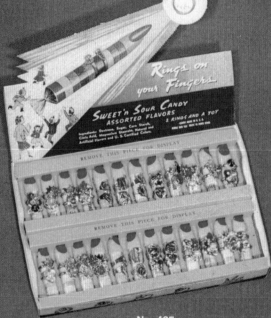

No. 403
MOONDROPS
—24 Count Display Box
Packed: 24 Boxes Per Case

No. 405
RINGS ON YOUR FINGER
—24 Count Display Box
Packed: 60 Boxes Per Case

1950s advertisements show the Ce De line-up, including 5-cent Popeye Cigarettes and the wearable candy rings and necklaces.

Chase and Poe Candy

In 1876, Dr. George Washington Chase was a struggling doctor, facing a quandary. While St. Joseph, Missouri, was an eventful Midwest river town, George was not supporting his family on his meager physician's wages. He decided that some extra income would help, so he opened a fruit and produce business. His son, who may have had a bit of a sweet tooth, influenced him to offer confections at their family grocery store.

G.W. Chase relinquished practicing medicine and soon had himself a thriving candy business. Chase Candy became known for its tasty sweets and rapidly had a loyal Midwest following. Around 1918, Chase launched what was to become the best-selling cherry candy bar in the country, Cherry Mash.

Cherry Mash was a hefty quarter-pound mound of chopped roasted peanuts blended with chocolate coating over a smooth cherry-fondant center. In the 1920s in order to keep up with the candy demand, Chase built a modern four-story factory in downtown St. Joseph. About this time the third generation of the Chase family, Charles, joined the company.

By 1925, with a history of 50 years of candy making, Chase had made countless candies, including an extensive line of candy bars. Chase's "Candy Cop" mascot helped sell bars like Pierce Arrow, T'ween Meals, Malted Milk, Chasenut, and the pervasive Cherry Mash. The company had a few disappointments, too. Opera Stick, Mammy's Pride, and Candy Dogs were a few that weren't produced for long.

Candy bar wrappers and packaging from Bunte, Chase, and Shotwell candy companies from the 1920s and 1930s. Under the Chase umbrella, these companies collectively produced hundreds of various candies.

While the Depression years were harsh on business, by the 1940s commerce was booming again for Chase. Profits had recovered and positioned Chase Candy as a lucrative investment for the F.S. Yantis and Company.

Yantis purchased Chase Candy in 1944 for over one million dollars. With the Yantis takeover, Chase began a series of acquisitions that within a few years made it one of the giants of the confectionery industry. Chase soon owned O'Brien, National, Shotwell, and the Nutrene Candy Companies. Then in 1954, Chase acquired Bunte Brothers Candy Company. Bunte was famous for fruit-filled hard candy called Diana Stuft Confections and a popular candy bar called Tango. All production of Bunte-Chase Candy was moved to Chicago. By the end of the 1950s, the candy conglomerate had sales over $14 million.

But the gigantic acquisitions proved to be overwhelming for a small-town candy company. The Chicago plant was closed by 1961. Chase Candy and the Cherry Mash returned home to St. Joseph.

Keeping it in the family, Chase merged with Poe Candy Company, which was started by a former Chase employee. So after big adventures in business and much candy later, Chase is back where they started — making their premier candy bar, Cherry Mash, the best-selling cherry bar in the country.

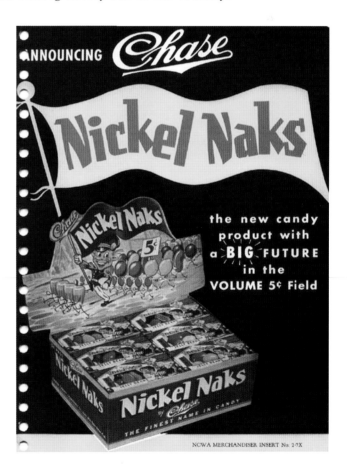

Doscher's

Famous for its taffy and canes, Doscher's has been in the candy business for 130 years. Established in 1871, Doscher's signature piece is a starchy, sugar-coated, vanilla taffy piece called the French Chew Taffy. Following four generations of family involved in running the company, the semi-retired Harry, Sr., and his son, Harry, Jr., are now at the helm. In addition to the famous taffy piece, the Doscher's Candy Company makes over 500,000 peppermint candy canes every year.

Claus Doscher, a German immigrant, started the company. Claus was in the sugar wholesale business before he went on to manufacture sweet items. He originally produced and sold a caramel popcorn product akin to Cracker Jack to the Cincinnati Red's ballpark. Claus Doscher then went into retailing sweets and started making his candy at a store in downtown Cincinnati. Not too far from their candy ancestry, today's current candy factory is located across the street from where a Depression-era Doscher's plant once stood.

The French Chew Taffy, created in 1902, was perhaps named after Turkish Taffy. The French Chew is technically nougat, not taffy, as the sugar mix is whipped and not pulled. French Chew was sold in big pieces that were broken up once they reached the store, where it was then sold by the pound. Now, it is produced in a few flavors and packaged in a long bar with a wrapper depicting a pleased candy-eating kid, licking his lips.

At first, French Chew's main competition was the popular Bonomo's Taffy, the first taffy to have a national sponsor. The Bonomo brand was bought by Tootsie in the 1970s and subsequently discontinued, leaving the French Chew without many direct taffy contenders.

An engineer by training, Harry, Jr., recently introduced a new piece of machinery to the established business, a bar cutter to cut the taffy evenly. Harry, Jr., is all for modernizing the operation while his father, who grew up cutting the taffy bars by hand, is less interested in updates. Even with technology advancements, the Doschers work long and hard to continue producing their legendary treats. An average candy day starts before 7 a.m. and may include managing brokers, answering phones, shipping out orders, and overseeing operations. Harry Doscher, Jr., also must conduct quality checks by pulling warm candy off the manufacturing line in the candy factory.

Sampling this classic taffy fresh from the factory must be a magnificent part of his job. Some like it hot but others prefer it cold. Doscher's taffy is also known as a good eat — straight from the freezer. Some think bars are best when frozen for a few hours and then cracked into pieces. Warm or cold, the French Chew Taffy, with its dusting of confectioners sugar, really pleases the palate.

Doscher's Cincinnati store in the early years.

1930s French Chew wrapper.

1950s French Chew wrapper.

Doscher's delivery truck, 1920s.

Ferrara Pan Company

The Ferrara Pan Company is known for its lively, mouth-puckering Lemonhead candies. Their super-hot Atomic Fireball was a predecessor in the now-popular intense candy category. Ferrara Pan also makes such familiar treats as Red Hots, Jaw Busters, and the well-loved, peanut-centered Boston Baked Bean.

Panned candies are coated candies made in a rotating pan. As their name implies, these candies are the company's specialty. This panning process involves building candy pieces from a single substance, such as nuts or candy centers, then tossing them in big revolving copper pans, while watchfully adding the flavor, color, and other candy ingredients. This panning process continues until the pieces grow to just the right size. When nearly finished, the candy gets a polish with an edible vegetable wax, which gives it a gloss and shine.

In 1900, Salvatore Ferrara came to America from Nola, Italy, and founded Ferrara Pan Candy Company in 1908. At the time of his immigration, Mr. Ferrara was a confectioner, skilled in the art of making Italian pastries and sugar-coated candy almonds. Sugar-coated candy almonds are otherwise known as "confetti" in Italy and other parts of Europe. These candy-coated almonds are also called Jordan almonds or almond dragees, and they continue to be a tradition at many weddings and celebrations. Early on, when they were covered with white sugar, they were a candy that symbolized purity and fertility.

By 1904, Salvatore Ferrara had become proficient in English and was settling into the thriving Chicago-Italian community. Because of his fluency in both English and Italian, he was soon working for the Santa Fe Railroad as an interpreter for crews and their foreman. He worked in rail transportation for several years and by 1908 opened a small Italian traditional pastry and confection shop in Chicago. From 1908 to 1919, the sugar-coated almond business grew. Ferrara was soon shipping his classic, always fresh, and in-demand product throughout the Midwest.

In 1919, Salvatore Ferrara, Salvatore Buffardi, and Anello Pagano, all brothers-in-law, realized the growing potential of panning not just almonds but a variety of other nut and flavored centers. They formed a partnership and began producing a wide assortment of confections. They constructed a manufacturing facility

Ferrara Pan's Atomic Fireballs were some of the first super-hot cinnamon candies.

ATOMIC fire ball

REG. U. S. PAT. OFF NO. 614,947

WITH THE RED HOT FLAVOR

on Taylor Street in Chicago's now-famous Italian neighborhood center. This early candy facility is the site where the original Ferrara Bakery is still located.

Ferrara Pan's classic cinnamon imperials or Red Hots, little red bits of sugary heat, were developed in 1932. These treats continue to adorn cupcakes and gingerbread houses. Red Hots sugar-and-spice blend is well-matched, creating a pellet of perfection.

In 1962, Lemonheads, little yellow citrus sour treats, were launched. They would spawn an entire line of fruity candies like the highly memorable but racially insensitive Cherry Chan. Cherry Chan was later renamed Cherryheads. The cherry candies were packaged in a bright red box featuring a sinister Asian fellow with a mustache. For a while, they were also named Cherry Clan and featured a trio of cherries with slanted eyes wearing rattan hats. Alexander the Grape and Mister Melon also got a name changes in order to fit in with Ferrara's branding strategy. All of the fruit candy items are currently referred to as "heads."

With his pointy nose and comb-over hairdo, Mr. Lemonhead helped launch an anti-drug message in the 1980s. "Don't be a Lemonhead, Say Nope to Dope!" was printed on Lemonhead boxes.

The same families — Ferrara, Buffardi, and Pagano — descendants of the founders, still own and manage the Ferrara Pan Candy Company. The candy has revised names and updated packaging, but their yummy taste has stood the test of time. Ferrara Pan's candies remain classic favorites.

Vintage Ferrara Pan Boxes.

Frank Fleer Gum Company

In the late 1800s when chewing gum was gaining popularity, Frank Fleer and his brother Henry experimented with making gum from chicle, the sticky substance from the sapodilla tree. The sap was tasteless but decidedly chewy and made for a decent piece of chewing gum. The brothers realized that, like most things, it was even better when coated with sugar. Soon, their small, white, candy-coated gum called Chiclets were sold by the scoop in drugstores and candy shops.

The Fleer brothers were very successful with their Chiclets gum, but it was popular mainly with adults. Frank aspired to make a gum that would appeal to children. In 1906, he developed a gum called Blibber-Blubber. His synthetic gum, however, was far too sticky and brittle to become a proper bubble gum and was never marketed.

The challenge to develop a commercial gum product for kids was not forgotten. The Frank H. Fleer Gum Company was eventually run by Frank Fleer's son-in-law Gilbert Mustin, and the quest for a popular blowing gum for children continued.

Walter Diemer, an accountant for the Frank Fleer Company, played in the company laboratory in his spare time. He came up with a stretchy mix that worked as a bubble gum — for one night anyway. When Walter Diemer came back to work the next day the gum was ruined. The sappy lump would barely stretch and would not produce any bubbles.

(Top) Walter Diemer.

(Middle) Photo by Tamara Staples From the gum collection of Jeff Nelson.

(Right) Dubble Bubble comic featuring Pud, circa 1960s.
Courtesy Concord Confections

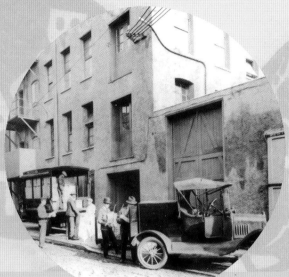

Black and white advertisement: A Fleer advertisement from Life Magazine 1951.

"THERE'S NO BUBBLE LIKE DUBBLE BUBBLE"*

*in other words: "PEOPLE ALL OVER THE WORLD HAVE FUN CHEWING FLEER'S DUBBLE BUBBLE GUM"

FLEERS DUBBLE BUBBLE GUM ®

1¢

FUNNIES, FORTUNES, FACTS ON EVERY WRAPPER!

FRANK H. FLEER CORP. PHILADELPHIA 41, PA.

Blast off, kids...

send today
for your new

DUBBLE
BUBBLE

SPACE SQUADRON

SPACE

HELMET!

FLEER DUBBLE BUBBLE ®

Guaranteed by Good Housekeeping

Mail this coupon today

AYS ASK FOR
DUBBLE BUBBLE
THE LARGE
PIECE THAT
VS BIGGER
LES

Here's how to get yours..

Be the first in your neighborhood to get your DUBBLE BUBBLE Space Helmet. Just follow instructions on coupon below and *mail today!* Hurry — supply is limited! Have your friends get one and form your own Space Squadron. Get extra coupons at the store where you buy Fleer DUBBLE BUBBLE Gum . . . The gum with the long-lasting secret flavour. Comics, facts and fortune in every piece!

SPACE HELMET
BOX 1585
TORONTO, ONTARIO

Enclosed is 25 cents in coin and 4 outside wrappers from Fleer DUBBLE BUBBLE Gum. Please send me my Space Helmet right away!

NAME
(print clearly)

ADDRESS

CITY/TOWN   PROV.

Form your own Space Squadron – Dubble Bubble space helmet advertisement, 1953.
Courtesy Concord Confections

Fleer Gum ad, 1940s
Dan Goodsell Collection

After a months of trying to reformulate another batch of blowable gum, the untrained scientist finally had a success. He found a recipe that produced big bubbles and easily peeled away after they burst. However, because he was working on the fly, he nearly forgot the food coloring necessary to brighten up the gray gob. The color on hand the day the formula worked just happened to be pink. After its launch in 1928, Fleer's Dubble Bubble became the top-selling one-cent confection. For years to come, Fleer would produce more than half of all the bubble gum American children were chewing. Most classic bubble gum has remained pink ever since.

Aside from achieving the first successful bubble gum, Fleer was the first company to wrap a comic called Fleer Funnies around a chunk of gum. The company developed twin characters called Dub and Bub, but as comedic competition from Bazooka Joe, Topps Chewing Gum's comic persona, stiffened, the twins were soon refined into one character called Pud. Vintage Fleer Funnies featuring the adventures of Pud, lucky fortunes, and a blurb of facts are highly collectible today.

Fleer launched its first bubble gum cards in 1923 with the general interest "Famous Pictures" set depicting landscapes and points of curiosity. In 1935 the company packaged a very pulp-fiction-sounding set called "Cops and Robbers," depicting famous hoodlums and their captors. It wasn't until the 1960s that they began covering sports figures. Fleer remains a player in sports-card collectables.

Today, bubble gum has become as American as apple pie, and Fleer, still churning out the pink plaster, continues to prove that bubble gum is no passing fad full of air. North American kids alone spend almost half a billion dollars on bubble gum every year. With that much gum, millions of bubbles must be blown every day. Pink bubbles are here to stay.

Gilliam Candy Company

Batter Up. The BB in BB Bats is for bigger, better.

Kits are the miniature square taffies, individually wrapped, in banana, peanut butter, chocolate, and strawberry flavors. They were originally wrapped with a machine that was developed not for sweet candy but for salty bouillon cubes.

BB Bats are the wonderfully nostalgic chewy taffy lollipops that come in strawberry, chocolate, banana, and molasses peanut flavors. They are the taffy pops that picture on the wrapper the old-fashioned baseball player up to bat. The suckers are called BB Bats not because the candy on a stick resembles a baseball bat. The BB actually stands for "bigger and better."

Slo Pokes are the delicious caramel slabs on a stick. Are they named for the fact that they are long-lasting or because they can possibly poke an eye out? One thing is for sure: these taffy favorites inevitably end up in the Halloween bag. But where do they come from?

In 1927, Cleve Gilliam opened the Candy Kitchen in Paducah, Kentucky. His little town store sold hard candy, stick candy, and peanut brittle. He and his few employees also made a line of good ole Kentucky Blue Grass nickel candy bars. He was an experienced candy crafter who received his training from nearby candy makers, including Standard Candy Company. Nashville's Standard Candy made the Goo Goo Cluster famous. The Goo Goo was the first combination candy bar comprised of multiple ingredients, all covered in chocolate.

With Gilliam's valuable candy experience, his little business prospered and soon his five employees grew to 95. His candy was reaching such far away places as Evansville, Indiana, and St. Louis, Missouri. In the 1930s, Cleve expanded his offerings to include square-meal-sounding candy bars. He had a line of candy with names like Bacon Slice, Tummy Full, and Cello Sally. While the business sustained, it wasn't until 1986 that things really got going. In 1986, James Lacy purchased Gilliam Candy. He added the classic duo of Kits and BB Bats, both produced since the 1920s, to Gilliam Candy in 1990.

Then, the Slo Poke brand was acquired in 1998. Slo Poke was a Holloway product, a sister to Milk Duds and Black Cows. Gilliam started making both the Slo Poke suckers as well as bite-size Slo Poke Caramels. Today, Gilliam continues to make the old-fashioned candies that Cleve built his business on. They also produce Sophie Mae Candies, another oldie goodie that uses recipes dating back to 1884.

Now, the classic taffy trios, along with the other Gilliam favorites, are available to customers who remember the great nostalgic candy from the 1940s, 1950s, or 1960s — as well as to a whole new generation of fans.

Gimbal's Fine Candies

Gimbal's Fine Candies has been producing their sweet stuff for over 100 years. Alexander Gimbal's father, Henry, was a forty-niner who came to California from France looking for gold. He did well in the gold mining business and soon developed grocery stores along the California stagecoach routes. Henry encouraged and helped his sons to take advantage of the growing Northern California region.

Heeding his father's entrepreneurial advice, Alexander Gimbal bought an existing candy company in 1898. Soon his two brothers, Louis and Eugene, were working with him. The bustling San Francisco downtown location offered the brothers many patrons who were eager for their delicious handmade candy. The brothers struck it rich — in candy.

The Gimbal brothers were innovators from the beginning. They used new technology like steam cookers to perfect their candy. Their original store advertised with a sign that read "Pacific Steam Candy Factory." In the initial years, their business became so popular that they had to move their facility several times to accommodate the growth.

The Gimbal brothers' factory got a shake up in 1906, the year of the great San Francisco earthquake. The factory was located on Washington and Montgomery Streets. To stop the fires that ravagedthe city after the quakes, dynamite was used to destroy anything standing. The Gimbal factory was located down the street from a U.S. customs house that could not be destroyed, and therefore the candy factory was spared. After the earthquake, Gimbal Brothers remained one of the only candy operations left in San Francisco. They were so busy that they found it hard to keep up with the demand.

The Depression hit the Gimbal Brothers Candy factory hard, but the only year the company operated at a loss was in 1932.

Business was barely up and running again when a great opportunity came in the late 1930s. The 1939 World's Fair was located on Treasure Island off of San Francisco's coast. San Francisco operated a ferry from downtown to Oakland and had also just finished construction on the Bay Bridge. The fair was well attended. It drew travelers, show-goers, and science seekers from all over the world. Gimbal Brothers took advantage of the opportunity by offering a "Candy Day," featuring free candy distributed by glamorous ladies. Sally Rand, a famous dancer, promoted the Gimbal Brothers candy in between waves of her feathered fan.

By the 1950s, Raynor, Jr., and Leroy, Jr., the third generation of Gimbals, were helping with the business. The company was advertising pieces like French Creams and Fruit Slices.

Today, the company continues to be led by a Gimbal along with his family and dedicated employees. Lance Gimbal represents the fourth generation in the business. Candies like Jelly Beans, Gummy Mummies, and Fruit Slices are the top sellers. Candy recipes, equipment, and factory locations have changed, but the steam process the company has used since the beginning is still in place.

Gimbal's fine products are found in both local drugstores and also in bigger stores like the classic West Coast candy shop See's Candy.

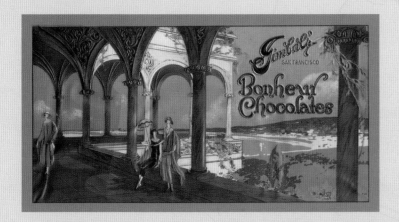

1920s Gimbal's candy catalog and boxes.

Gimbal Brothers has offered San Franciscan's premiere candies since 1898. These deluxe boxes are from the 1920s and are highly collectible.

Gimbal's — corner of First and Folsom Streets, San Francisco, where the finest candy specialties in the West are made There is no substitute for experience. The resources and methods of this institution have been developed through a quarter of a century's successful candy manufacture

Caramel Cream.

Goetze's Candy Company

In 1895, August Goetze, a German immigrant, began manufacturing a variety of confections in his small Baltimore, Maryland, candy plant. The company was started as the Baltimore Chewing Gum Company, and its main candy product was just that, gum. However, as bigger and more powerful businesses entered into the world of candy, Goetze was forced out by the rising cost of chicle. Big-time gum competitors were buying chicle plantations in Mexico and controlling the cost of the necessary gum ingredient. The Goetze company had to explore other candy prospects.

In the early 1940s, after hard Depression years, wars, and rising costs, Goetze decided to focus his attention on the manufacturing of one item that would be the industry model of consistency and quality. The goal led the company to manufacture its signature piece, the Caramel Cream, exclusively. Also called the Bull's Eye Caramel, this piece has a delicious cream center, almost like a dollop of fresh cream, to accompany the chewy caramel.

In 1958, the company was incorporated under the name Goetze's Candy Company, Inc. Today, the company is located in the same building that housed the original manufacturing plant in 1928. Production has grown and the building has expanded, but the same dedication to quality candy has prevailed for more than 100 years.

The Goetze Company, after all these years and trends in candy, still produces one of the finest and only caramel creams in the country. The firm has progressed from horse-and-cart deliveries around downtown Baltimore to large shipments that reach destinations such as Europe, Asia, and even Australia.

The company manufactures a few variations on its first caramels, different packages and assortments, but the recipe for the classic, beloved piece is the same. You'll also find the Caramel Cream in a long skinny version called a Cow Tale. It's is a delicious rope of caramel filled with the white cream. Currently run by Mitchell Goetze and his brother Todd, the company celebrated its 100th birthday in 1995. Goetze's Candy Company continues the sweet and lovely candy tradition started by their family four generations ago.

Goetze "Pepsin" Gum factory around the turn of the 20th century.

Goldenberg Candy Company

Rich molasses, combined with sugar and freshly roasted Georgia peanuts, makes for a fine combination. Cover that with a layer of the best dark chocolate and you have a confection masterpiece. The Goldenberg's Peanut Chew is all that.

David Goldenberg arrived in Philadelphia from Romania in 1880 to start a new life. By 1890, he had taught himself how to cook sugar items and was selling them to local carnivals and fairs. With his business a success, he eventually opened a small retail candy store. He sold lollipops, cotton candy, caramels, and a handmade chewy walnut and molasses candy, originally called a Walnut Roll. The small family-owned business was a local favorite for years. The entire family worked in the business and lived above the store. The candy recipes varied and times changed. The Walnut Roll eventually became a peanut roll when manufacturing with walnuts became too expensive.

The Goldenbergs got a contract with the military to send their product overseas and a whole new world, literally, of Peanut Chew consumers opened up. In fact, recently a Goldenberg Peanut Chew box from the 1940s showed up in a book published by the Jewish Museum in Berlin. During wartime, the American candy was a great treat for the soldiers. In addition, the sturdy and classically American box was a nice keepsake. Incidentally, the Goldenberg Peanut Chew box is in the Berlin museum, donated by someone who kept passport photos of Jewish forced laborers in the candy box. The photo collection, Goldenberg Peanut Chew box and all, was donated to the Jewish Museum in 1980.

After WWII, the American candy business was saturated with small companies. Without big army contracts, competition was tough. When David was ready to retire in the late 1940s, his children, Harry and Sylvia, bought the Peanut Chew division, by then a top-selling favorite. They began the handmade manufacturing of the delicious piece out of a converted garage in Penna, Pennsylvania. The little chew originally was a full candy bar and went to bite-size pieces when the company decided that moviegoers may want a small-size candy treat that was easy to nibble on during a feature film. Harry's two children, Carl and Ed, continued the candy tradition, selling their Peanut Chew piece to concession stands, vending companies, and supermarkets in the Northeast, growing the Peanut Chew market. Then two of their children, David and Mindy, became the fourth generation of Goldenbergs to operate the candy business. The company continued to make the Peanut Chew exclusively; however, now it comes in all shapes and sizes to please the different candy retailers.

Recently, Just Born Candy Company, makers of Hot Tamales, Mike and Ikes, and Peeps, purchased the Goldenberg Company to add to their nostalgic classics. They might choose to update the candy wrapper slightly, but they have vowed to continue to make close to two million of the classic Peanut Chew pieces per day. The Goldenberg candy tradition has not been lost. And you know it when you taste one.

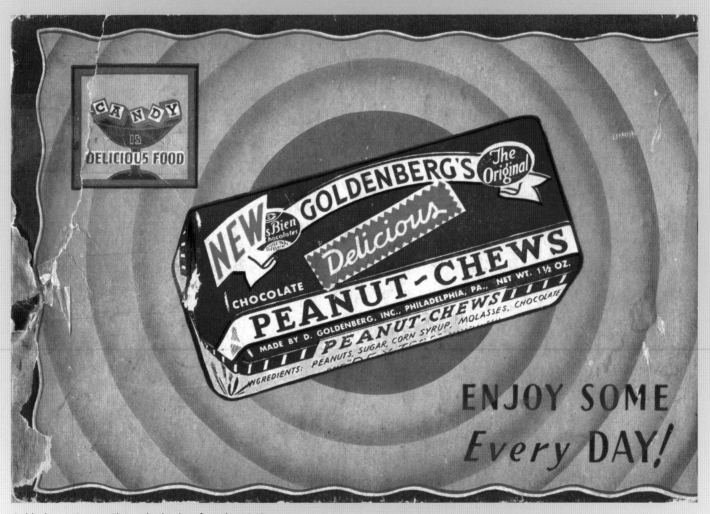

Goldenberg's Peanut Chews display box from the 1940s.
Goldenberg Candy Company

Hammond's Candies

Hammond's Candies Denver store in the 1940s.

Classic and beautiful hard candies, ribbon candy, and lollipops have been made at Hammond's Candies since 1920. Their crystal cuts are made almost the same way a professional artisan would cut glass. Their ribbon candies and lollipops are equally spectacular works, with bright colors and great flavors. Each candy piece painstakingly produced is a miniature work of art.

Carl T. Hammond began to make candy when he was only 14 years old, preferring the creative and hard work of crafting candy over school. He worked as an apprentice for several local Denver area candy makers before enlisting in the U.S. Army during World War I. Upon returning, he realized that he missed the confection business he had trained in. He started his own sweets factory in 1920.

Hammond's crystal-cut candies are miniature artworks.

110

Hammond's lollipops and ribbon candy are handmade with a process unchanged for more than 80 years.

Hammond's started out as a small candy producer, selling mostly to Denver area businesses. The firm grew big enough to expand its factory space but never too big to compromise quality; Hammond's candy remains handmade.

Carl Tom Hammond, Jr., worked for his father and eventually took over the family business. Tom and his wife June were second-generation owners. A third-generation Hammond ran the show until he recently retired.

Making Hammond's candy is not easy. Hard candy starts out as a 340-degree sugary liquid in a 30-gallon copper kettle. After heating, the thick liquid is poured on to a table to cool. Each batch, weighing about 60 pounds, is then worked to beautify and structure the candy. Stripes are formed through pulling, kneading, or "blocking" the cooled candy mass by hand. Throughout the process, flavors are added. Then the candy is pulled further to obtain the proper consistency and color. The candy is then spun into a thick rope to be whirled into a lollipop, cut into a classic stick, or shaped into a candy cane. There are about 900 small lollipops in each batch, so after the hard work of shaping and cutting, sticks and wrappers are applied to each individual piece. From cooking to finished product, each candy batch takes an hour.

Because Hammond's product remains handmade, while other manufacturers have moved to machines, the company has carved out a special niche in the big world of candy. Today, many candy canes and lollipops are mass-produced. Hammond's now sells its unique specialty candy to national retailers, catalogs, and small shops alike. They are the largest distributor of handmade hard candy in America. Hammond's Candies, totally dedicated to tradition, is unwilling to automate their production. The company's stunning candy continues to be produced exactly as it was 84 years ago.

Hershey Chocolate Company

Henry Hershey, a Mennonite farmer, inventor, and dreamer, once produced cough drops that he claimed were far better than the Smith Brothers'. His claims went unfounded and no business lasted very long for Henry. His schemes did keep his family moving, always looking for the next big thing. His son Milton attended seven schools before the age of fourteen. He finally dropped out in fourth grade, never to return again.

Milton, weary of his fathers failures, set out for Philadelphia to make his own hard candy line in 1882. Familiar with the candy industry from his four years as an apprentice, he was still a little uncertain of how to master it. When his own candy business did not pan out, Milton tried confection start-ups in other cities. Failure in both Philadelphia and New York did not deter him. Unlike his father, who was forever planning trips to faraway places to pan gold, Milton did not veer off into unfamiliar territories. He persevered in candy.

Milton Snavely Hershey then started over as a manufacturer of caramels. In 1886 he formed the Lancaster Caramel Company, which made wonderful-sounding pieces like Lotuses, Uniques, and Empires. Over the course of a few years, he made a small fortune, married, and even installed a very un-Mennonite fancy water fountain in his front yard. Things were looking up for Milton who, unlike his father, was finally mastering a trade.

He sold his thriving caramel business in 1900 at age 43 to risk everything on a new venture — chocolate. An 1892 visit to England enlightened the "Caramel King" when he saw the various ways chocolate could be used. Shortly after his European trip, his suspicions about chocolate were confirmed when he found newly developed chocolate bar equipment at the 1893 World's Colombian Exposition in Chicago. The fair displayed the latest and greatest machinery from around the globe. It was then and there he bought the new technology and had the German-made machines shipped to Lancaster. Once home, he experimented with various chocolate recipes and formulas before selling his caramel company. The company sold for $1 million dollars to the American Caramel Company, while the Paul F. Beich Company took part of Hershey's Chicago-area holdings. His chocolate machinery was not part of the deal. Hershey wisely maintained rights to produce chocolate.

Hershey, Pennsylvania — depicted here on a box of BonBons, circa 1930 — included parks, hotels and sports facilities.
Beth Kimmerle Collection

Hershey Aero Wrapper from the 1940s.
Beth Kimmerle Collection

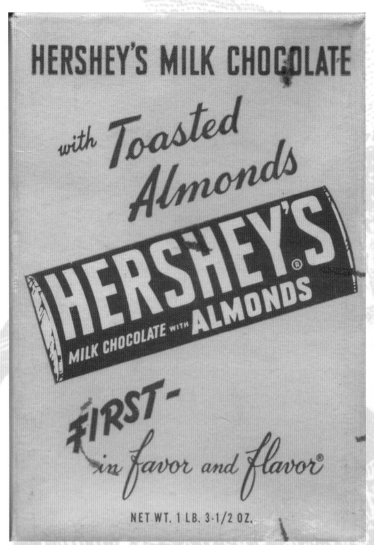

Hershey Milk Chocolate candy, one of the most recognized wrapers in the world, 1928.
Beth Kimmerle Collection

1940s Krackel wrapper.
Beth Kimmerle Collection

1940s Mr. Goodbar wrapper. Mr. Goodbar was launched in 1925.
Beth Kimmerle Collection

In 1903, Hershey broke ground on a new production facility in Derry Church, Pennsylvania, close to dairy farms and other fresh ingredients needed to produce his chocolate product. His plan was to mass-produce a high-quality, signature product and distribute it widely. By 1905, after his huge factory was complete, he began production of Hershey's Milk Chocolate Bar. In a matter of years, Milton's five-cent chocolate candy bar, made with the freshest milk and individually wrapped in a glossy chocolate-colored wrapper, was known and loved across America. Hershey's candy plan finally succeeded. Currently, Hershey's Chocolate Bar is one of the most recognized products in the world.

Hershey's factory quickly grew into a bustling town where Milton envisioned a chocolate utopia. He built houses for his workers, a transit system, a school, a hotel, stores, and a community center. By 1906, a post office was needed, and the town became officially recognized as Hershey, Pennsylvania.

In 1907, Hershey's Kisses were introduced. In 1921, Hershey added the slender glassine strip that identified his product from the mimickers. The kiss was named for the way the small dollop of extruded chocolate barely kissed the production belt. As it turned out, people loved not only the romantic connotations but the shimmery, silver-foil wrapper used to cover the conical confection. It proved to be a lasting addition.

The Mr. Goodbar candy bar hit the market in 1925. It was made from a slightly different chocolate formula and poured into a different mold. The bar was wider and a bit longer than the standard Hershey's Bar.

With its bright yellow wrapper and fresh peanuts nestled among the chocolate, it was an instant success. In 1917, Harry B. Reese was employee at the Hershey dairy farm. In 1923, Reese had set up his own small candy factory with Milton Hershey's blessing. He sold his finest creation, a chocolate cup filled with smooth, sweetened peanut butter, to his former employer in 1963. Hershey went on to make several products, including Reese's Pieces, from the original Reese peanut butter concept. Reese's Pieces had their film debut in Steven Spielberg's *E.T.* and from then on, sales have been out of this world.

By World War II, the candy maker was specially formulating bars to send overseas to soldiers. This became a steady business for the chocolate maker at a time when ingredients were rationed. In 1944 alone, Hershey shipped 4 million Ration D bars a week. Many of Hershey's fellow candy makers were forced to cease production entirely. Hershey's inclusion in Army rations resulted in many Europeans tasting their first Hershey Bar, oftentimes in a trench. A bar also made a great barter for other goods and services. G.I. drills had men checking that they were carrying ammunition — and a Hershey bar.

In the 1970s, the Kit Kat bar was added to the Hershey family when the company bought the rights to produce the British favorite from Rowntree Mackintosh. It was launched overseas as Chocolate Crisp and was renamed Kit Kat two years later.

Milton S. Hershey, the multi-millionaire, died penniless in 1945, as he left his entire fortune to a school for orphaned and disadvantaged children. He and his wife never had children and Hershey, who didn't have much education himself, placed high value on the education and future of impoverished children. Well endowed, Hershey's school has become a highly regarded institution, educating thousands and sending many students off to Ivy League schools.

In 2002, the school's trustees, owning 55 percent of the Hershey Chocolate Company, threatened to sell the company. When people expressed their outrage at the possible end of one of the last company communities, not to mention an American icon, the Hershey Trust backed down. For a moment, it seems the school forgot about Milton's quality of perserverence. And persevered he has. Milton Hershey brought chocolate to the masses, bringing what was once considered luxury item to the entire world.

In 2003, 100 years after the building of his Lancaster factory, Hershey continues to make many top-selling candy bars and candy including Twizzlers, Reese's, Mr. Goodbar, Payday, Almond Joy, York Mint, Whoppers, Rolo, and Hershey's Kisses. For generations, many have loved these classic candies. Topping the fine candy assortment list is the Hershey Milk Chocolate Bar.

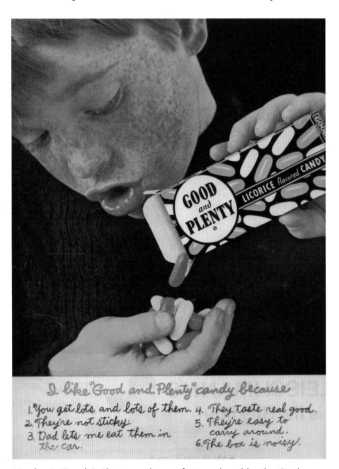

Hershey's Good & Plenty candy was first produced by the Quaker City Confectionery Company in Philadelphia in 1893 and is one of the oldest branded candies in the U.S.
Beth Kimmerle Collection

Hershey's candy bar offerings, 1940.
Dan Goodsell Collection

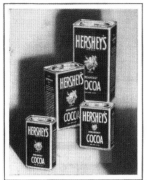

Additional to its rich chocolate flavor, HERSHEY'S Breakfast Cocoa is nourishing and easily digested. Owing to its concentrated nutriment it becomes, when milk is added, an almost perfect food

As a dainty confection, HERSHEY'S Milk Chocolate Kisses are unsurpassed

For baking purposes, HERSHEY'S Baking Chocolate is unequalled, adding an exquisite flavor to cakes and desserts

HERSHEY'S Milk Chocolate is known the world over for its velvety smoothness, delicate and characteristic flavor

HERSHEY'S Chocolate Syrup in an unopen can never gets hard or sugary. It makes a delicious and wholesome drink, hot or cold, and is an unexcelled topping for ice cream, puddings and desserts that would be improved by the addition of Chocolate flavor

HERSHEY'S Almond Bars are of marked individuality and superiority and are high in food value

Hershey products from *The Hershey Recipe Book*, 1928.
Michael Rosenberg Collection

Reese's Peanut Butter Cups, developed by former Hershey employee H.B. Reese, later spawned a series of popular peanut candies, including Reese's Pieces.
Michael Rosenberg Collection

Idaho Candy Company

A candy bar named for a vegetable is not very common. A candy bar named for a potato is truly rare. But there is one. The Idaho Spud has been in production since 1918. It was named for the potato because Idaho, where the candy hails from, produces lots of spuds, about a quarter of the total U.S. production to be exact. The Idaho Spud candy bar has no actual potato flavors in it, and it is much lighter than its starchy name-sake. It is made of fluffy marshmallow, covered in dark chocolate, and sprinkled with coconut. The hand-formed candy apparently looked a little like a lumpy chocolate covered potato when it was first made. Do not let the name daunt you; this potato-shaped candy is truly luscious.

To further honor their glorious region and its natural offerings, Idaho Candy Company makes a candy bar named for Old Faithful in nearby Yellowstone National Park. A perfectly wonderful geyser to name a candy bar after, this candy is comprised of chocolate-coated peanuts with a marshmallow center. This Old Faithful does not have a gushing candy center.

In addition to the unusual names they have chosen for the firm's candy, Idaho Candy Company uses the name Owyhee as a registered brand. Owyhee is the name of a river, a mountain range, and a county in Idaho named for the Owyhee Indians who explored the area.

T.O. Smith, the man responsible for creating the distinctive names, can also be credited with forming the delicious candy. He started as a hobby candy maker, crafting homemade chocolate items for his family and friends. As he became more skilled, his candy became better tasting and he decided to make a small business out of selling sweets. Around the turn of the century, he set up a small production in his garage and began to sell his chocolates locally. Before long, Smith built an official factory located in downtown Boise to accommodate his growing sales.

His modern candy-making facility had new innovations like skylights and offered progressive benefits such as a welfare room for employees. Over the years, this same factory produced many candies and chocolates including over 50 different types of candy bars.

Today, Idaho Candy Company is owned and operated by the Wagers family, a local area family that not only understands candy tradition but the significance of the unconventional names. Several of their best-selling candy bars are still produced by this established candy company, with a penchant for local and unusual names, in the original factory in Boise.

The current wrapper of the Idaho Spud, complete with potato eyes.

The modern Idaho Candy factory, complete with skylights and telephones, circa 1940.

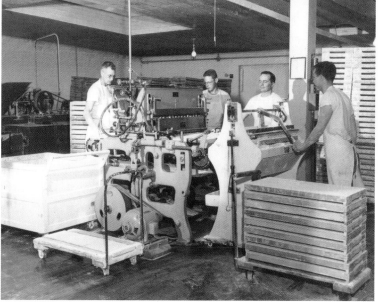

Jelly Belly Candy Company

Eight flavors of intensely flavored jelly beans were crafted in the summer of 1976. They were produced on request by a driver for a candy distributor who had a dream to create "the Rolls Royce of jelly beans."

The flavors were not standard; they were specially formulated and highly unusual for that time. Root beer and cream soda had never before been made into a jellybean. The name for the specialty beans was also novel. It came from a 1920s blues singer called Leadbelly. Jelly Belly's were sold as individual flavors, and the Goelitz Candy Company was soon selling them faster than it could make them. Orders for the yummy flavored beans were booked two years in advance.

The public adored them and clamored for more. Round-the-clock shifts at two separate factories worked overtime to supply the enormous demand. The company added more beans in additional flavors. After over 20 years, Jelly Belly Candy Company continues to produce an amazing little product with a following as intense as the flavors. Jelly Belly jellybeans can be found worldwide. They are truly an American candy produced by a company with a great American story.

In the late 1860s, two energetic brothers came to America from Germany. In a few short years, they had a thriving candy making business located in Belleville, Illinois. Gustav was the candy maker while his brother Albert sold their handmade candy to surrounding towns from a horse-drawn wagon.

The business prospered but before long the Panic of 1893 upset their imminent growth. The brothers went into bankruptcy and were forced to sell the business. Albert continued to sell candy. Gustav died in 1901.

By 1898 the economy was back on track and Gustav's sons continued on with the family business. Adolph Goelitz and a partner, William Kelley, opened a candy company and Adolph's two brothers soon joined them. The Ohio-based Goelitz Confectionery Company prospered. By 1912, the company was turning away business for lack of production capacity. They moved their operation to a larger factory in north Chicago where they could produce their mallocremes and other tasty candies. Goelitz Confectionery also became known for manufacturing the best and freshest candy corn or "chicken feed" available. They have continued to make the tri-colored kernels longer than any other manufacturer in candy industry.

Goelitz is famous for their "chicken feed" or candy corn.
Jelly Belly Collection

Former president Ronald Reagan, a jelly bean fan, was presented with over seven thousand pounds of Jelly Belly jellybeans for his inauguration.

To Bill Kelley
With best wishes,

Ronald Reagan

During World War I, Herman Goelitz pioneered a candy factory in the West, and soon two individual Goelitz factories were making candy. While the two companies thrived in the Roaring Twenties, the Depression years were especially hard. Hundreds of candy makers were closing their shops and facing bankruptcy. The Goelitz valuable and top-selling commodity, candy corn, had sold for 16 cents a pound in the heyday of the 1920s, but had dropped to 8 cents ten years later.

After the 1930s, things slowly returned to normal, and the company's delicious product was soon in demand again. A post-war boom saw demand up again after World War II. The candy business was vulnerable but the Goelitz Companies continued to produce through recessions and wars alike.

By the 1970s, a third generation entered into the confectionery business to manufacture candy corn and mellocreams. William Kelley in Chicago and his California cousin, Herman Rowland, both descendants of Gustav Goelitz, were now at the helm. While they were eager to expand their family business, high prices for sugar hurt the entire candy industry which was completely dependent on huge quantities of the sweet substance. The cousins muddled though the sugar crisis and by 1976 were united again, producing the biggest candy novelty the industry had seen in years.

Today the Goelitz Company is called the Jelly Belly Candy Company. They carry on the tradition that their ancestors started almost 150 years ago. You'll find their classics like candy corn along with new flavors of Jelly Belly jelly beans everywhere.

Goelitz candy catalog, 1920.
Jelly Belly Collection

Goelitz Brothers, Belleville, Illinois, candy storefront, circa 1900.

122

Just Born Candy Company

In 1910, Samuel Born, an immigrant from Russia, landed in the United States. Once in the land of opportunity, Born wasted no time. Shortly after his arrival, the mechanically-gifted and entrepreneurial Born invented a machine that inserted sticks into lollipops. By 1923, Sam Born had opened a small but thriving candy store in Brooklyn, New York. In his store window, he displayed his newly formed, fresh candy creations with a sign that invited the passersby to see what had been "Just Born!" that day. Sam's sign played on his last name and the freshness of his candy. The theme became a hit, and the company soon developed a logo of a small baby nestled in a candy scale.

When Born's brothers-in-law joined the thriving business, Born became free to work on his latest candy creations and inventions. While they ran the store and manufacturing, Born was busy creating chocolate Jimmies or Sprinkles and an air-hardening chocolate coating for ice cream. Many of Born's early inventions are still used in the candy and sweets business today.

Just Born's candy business continued to prosper despite the economic hardships during the Depression. In 1932, Just Born moved from Brooklyn to the company's current location on Newton Avenue in Bethlehem, Pennsylvania. The company, rich with opportunity, attracted lines of applicants looking for jobs. The company continued to grow by making excellent fresh candy along with purchasing other smaller candy makers. The addition of Maillard Candy added hand-decorated chocolates, crystallized fruits, Venetian mints, and bridge mix to their line-up.

In 1953, Just Born acquired the Rodda Candy Company of Lancaster, Pennsylvania. Rodda specialized in Easter products. They made jellybeans and a small line of marshmallow products. Of special interest was a hand-made marshmallow chick called a "Peep." During their early years, these

1950s Peeps, when they had wings and were individually formed.

original Marshmallow Peeps were squeezed, one at a time, out of a pastry tube. The eyes were painted on by hand, and they had little attached wings. Back in the day, one little chick Peep took hours to make.

Sam Born's innovative character was inherited by his son Robert, who joined the company in 1946. The young Born, with his plant manager, mechanized the marshmallow forming process. Robert Born later was company president for over 30 years and went on to develop many more manufacturing advances. As a result, he helped build Just Born into the world's largest manufacturer of fluffy marshmallow treats, producing as many as 3.8 million Marshmallow Peeps and Bunnies of various pastel colors every day.

In the 1950s, Just Born utilized Rodda's jelly bean expertise by introducing several new products, including spicy, cinnamon-flavored Hot Tamales and the classic fruit-flavored Mike and Ikes. They also recently introduced Zours, a super-tart candy bean. In the 1960s, the company dropped its chocolate line to concentrate on its current marshmallow and panned candy offerings. After ten years of working alongside their fathers, Ross Born and his cousin, David Shaffer, became Just Born's co-presidents in 1992. Just as leadership of the company has been multi-generational, so has the work force. Many of the more than 450 Just Born employees are third-generation candy makers.

In 2000, the state recognized Just Born as one of the best places to work in all of Pennsylvania. Today, Just Born is the top maker of marshmallow confections in the United States, with the yummy pastel Marshmallow Peeps and Bunnies hailed as the top-selling nonchocolate Easter candy.

Sam Born, candy engineer, circa 1910

Bob Born, 1953.

The bright yellow marshmallow Peep has been an Easter staple for years.
Just Born Candy Archives

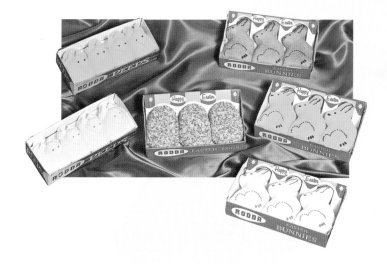

Hot Tamales, Jolly Joes, and Mike and Ikes were all "born" in the 1950s.
Dan Goodsell Collection

M&M Mars

Frank C. Mars was making chocolates and butter cream candies in the kitchen of his small Tacoma, Washington, home in 1911. It was not the first time he had tried his hand at the confection business. The urge to succeed in candy had brought him to many U.S. cities and into debt. Nine years later, at the age of 37, he moved his small-time candy-making operation to Minneapolis, where he and his second wife took a room above their tiny candy shop called The Nougat House. With a few failures behind him and plenty of experience, Frank began to think bigger, experimenting with candies he could manufacture on a large scale and distribute throughout the nation.

The Mar-O-Bar candy bar, Frank's first true candy bar attempt, was not an instant hit. However, in 1923, he tried another combination bar, built from a few delicious ingredients, and called it a Milky Way. The candy was much larger than the Hershey's Milk Chocolate Bar, offering lots of perceived value. The candy bar stayed fresh with a chocolate coating that sealed the caramel and aerated nougat filling. It could be shipped across the country and still stay on store shelves for days.

Forrest E. Mars, Frank's son, maintained that the idea for the Milky Way bar came to him while sharing a milkshake with his father. He recommended the chocolate malt flavor, believing it might be great for a candy. While it is hard to know where the idea came from, it is certain that the candy bar changed the way people thought about and bought candy forever. Mars would help the country and later the world move from simple chocolate to various combinations of caramel, nuts, and nougat.

Business grew and soon Mars, Inc. needed a larger factory. In 1928, Frank opened a grand Spanish-style manufacturing facility in Chicago's Oak Park. His son joined him in business at the busy Chicago plant but only for a short while. When their business styles clashed, Frank sent Forrest off to open up European markets with their successful Milky Way bar. Forest sweetened the formula for British tastes and called his Euro Milky Way a Mars Bar.

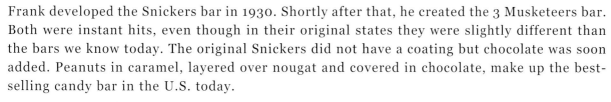

Frank developed the Snickers bar in 1930. Shortly after that, he created the 3 Musketeers bar. Both were instant hits, even though in their original states they were slightly different than the bars we know today. The original Snickers did not have a coating but chocolate was soon added. Peanuts in caramel, layered over nougat and covered in chocolate, make up the best-selling candy bar in the U.S. today.

The early 3 Musketeers bar was actually comprised of three mini-pieces: chocolate, vanilla, and strawberry. When the fresh ingredients for strawberry became costly to produce, the 3 Musketeers were made into one bar.

With a complete lineup of top sellers, Frank Mars's candy company was successful. In 1932, with sales at more than $25 million, second in the candy line only to Hershey, Frank Mars finally had himself a thriving candy business.

1930s black-and-white 3 Musketeers advertisement.

3 Musketeers were originally three distinct pieces – vanilla, strawberry, and chocolate flavored.

Michael Rosenberg Collection

INDIAN PRAIRIE PUBLIC LIBRARY
401 Plainfield Road
Darien, IL 60561

Ping

For a Real Taste Thrill, try the New Cocoanut PING Sweet dark chocolate... crisp shredded cocoanut... and soft smooth nougat.

PACKED 24 BARS TO THE BOX

MARS

For the Finest Quality Candy Bar of them all, try the Mars Toasted Almond Bar Extra thick pure milk chocolate ...crisp toasted almonds... snowy-white nougat center.

PACKED 24 BARS TO THE BOX

MARS PRODUCTS ASSORTMENT

MPA

The entire Mars line in a box of 42 bars — a complete assortment of the Mars line available in one box — assorted as follows:

12 — 5c MILKY WAY
6 — 10c MARS
6 — 5c SNICKERS
6 — 5c FOREVER YOURS
4 — 5c PING
8 — 5c 3 MUSKETEERS

PACKED 42 BARS TO THE BOX

Forever Yours
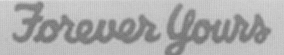

A 1938 Mars factory guidebook shows the complete Mars candy line-up.
Michael Rosenberg Collection

SNICKERS

A Trip Thru Mars

" We saw behind the scenes — "

128

Meanwhile, the displaced Forrest realized there were new markets for candy. He had moved to Europe and immersed himself in candy by training with chocolate makers across Europe. With his Yale University business background, he grew his Mars Bar business, while diversifying his company into various packaged goods like rice and dog food. Forrest was shrewd, striving for efficiencies and perfect product. He was a confident and strategic businessman with a commanding entrepreneurial drive. Forrest eventually took control of his father's Chicago-based Mars. He went on to combine their candy brands and built a lasting candy empire.

Forrest's big break came before his takeover in 1940 with the invention of M&M's. Upon returning from Europe, he developed the legendary colorful chocolate circle with an associate named Bruce Murrie. Forrest's inspiration was a candy-coating process that prevented chocolates from melting. Bruce had chocolate in his family lineage as well. His father, William, worked for Milton Hershey and was one of his closest friends. The initials M&M's stand for Mars and Murrie. The candies debuted in 1941 and became a favorite of GIs serving in World War II. First packaged in cardboard tubes, the bright little dots were welcomed and appreciated by privates and the public alike.

M&M's Peanut came out in 1954 and the cheery colored pellets became one of America's favorite candies. The company dropped red M&M's in 1976 when there was some controversy surrounding a red dye used to color food. With the slogan, "The Milk Chocolate Melts in your mouth-not in your hands," red M&M's were reinstated in the 1980s when the dyes were proved to be safe, much to consumers' delight.

Fully realizing how committed consumers were to chocolate and the color it comes in, the company asked loyal customers to vote for an additional color in 1995. Blue won over pink and purple by a landslide.

Now, the brightly colored M&M's are just a small part of the Mars candy rainbow. M&M's, Snickers, Milky Way, 3 Musketeers, Mars Bar, Twix, Starburst — they all lead to the pot o' gold. And candy is only part of the company. Mars still owns interests in pet food and rice and has added ice cream treats, like the Dove Bar, and other snacks, like the cheese-filled pretzel Combos, to their offerings.

The Mars family is routinely listed in Forbes as one of the richest in America. The Mars conglomerate has global sales in the billions of dollars and is considered one of the largest privately held companies in the world. The candy business their father and grandfather built is now run by Forrest, Jr., and his brother, John. M&M Mars is still privately held, entrepreneurially operated, and highly secretive about their business — just like Wonka would have wanted.

CHOCOLATE
First bite, chocolate... pure Mars milk chocolate, poured on thick as it'll stay!

ALMONDS
Then crispy, whole almonds, the expensive kind, toasted till they're gold. Plenty of them!

NOUGAT
Rich, creamy nougat that comes from fresh egg whites and pure sugar, whipped till it's fluffy!

Like a Chocolate Nut Sundae!

Close those great big eyes

Just halfway, though. Now, for a moment, just let your imagination sink down through that elegant, double-thick, pure milk chocolate. Down into that luscious creamy, whipped, mellow nougat. Savor those big toasty, crunchy, golden almonds. Just like a chocolate nut sundae. Get a Mars Bar—take a big, mellow bite, and close those great big eyes. M-m-m.

★ MARS ®
Toasted Almond BAR 10¢

GREAT DAY FOR A TREAT...

Great way to start a great day—with a traditional treat like a Milky Way candy bar! Just taste that thick, milk chocolate coating ... the golden layer of smooth, creamy caramel ... and the soft, chocolate nougat center. Richly flavored with real malted milk. All blend together to make each enjoyable mouthful a real taste thrill ... right down to the last delightful flavor that lingers in your mouth. When you crave good candy, eat a

Milky Way

Big Chief of the Nickel Tribe

Three-flavored bargain from Mars' outfit! Milkiest ... the rest-blood chocolate-covered candy bar in all the world ...

Milky Way 5¢

130

it's the Chocolate— it's the Nougat— it's the Nuts!

MARS...the 3-flavor candy bar

Honest-to-goodness MILK CHOCOLATE   Creamy NOUGAT   Toasted whole ALMONDS

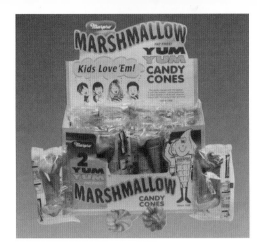

Marshmallow Cone Company

The Marshmallow Cone creator was a Cincinnati, Ohio-based tailor whose business had severely slumped with the hard times of the Depression. He realized that while people did not always have money to get their pants hemmed, they did seem to have a bit of spare change for a sweet treat. He decided to supplement his tailoring business by making an affordable penny candy product. He purchased a few cooking supplies, set up in the back of his shop, and started to teach himself the scientific candy craft. During the tough Depression years, John V. Arbino worked hard, making and mending clothes by day and concocting his marshmallow candy at night.

To get his product distributed, his early marshmallow treats were sold to local stores and bakeries on consignment, with retailers paying him as his popular product left the shelves. On weekends, John loaded up his car with his handmade marshmallow-shaped animals and sold his fresh fluff at local markets.

His business went well and survived the Depression years. The hardworking Arbino, a trained tailor, evolved into a professional confectioner, replacing his sewing machines with eggbeaters and copper pots. In the 1950s, when the overwhelming popularity of ice cream threatened to infringe on his own sweets, the candy maker produced a multicolored marshmallow swirl in a cone. The candy cones were an instant hit, piggybacking on the popularity of ice cream. Unlike ice cream, however, the fun marshmallow candy cones did not need to be cooled and were loved all year long. Word spread about his creative cones and eventually the Ohio candy maker was sending his ice cream "clone" all over the country.

The other marshmallow shapes were eventually discontinued to make way for what the company promoted as "a tasty treat in a crispy cone." When John Arbino, Jr., took over the company in the 1960s, he updated the company by purchasing baking machines and automatic packaging lines. Today, the company continues to produce the classic cones with modern machinery. The firm has, however, maintained that nostalgic look and its Marshmallow Cone continues to delight old-timers and children alike.

Marshmallow cones resemble a mini ice cream cone but are easier to ship, store, and eat than their cold cousins.
Marpro Collection

assorted....or all chocolate
or all wintergreen....5¢

New England Confectionery Co., Cambridge 39, Mass.

NECCO

In 1847, after inventing and patenting the first American candy machine, a lozenge cutter, Oliver R. Chase and his brother founded a small candy company. Chase and Company would become the pioneer component of the later formed NECCO. Between 1850 and 1876, the Chases continued to create machinery to produce their popular wafer candy. At the 1876 Centennial Exhibition in Philadelphia, the candy industry made an impressive demonstration, and Chase and Company was one of 20 firms exhibiting their high-tech candy equipment.

In the early 1880s, D. L. Clark began the manufacture of his own confectionery treats in the back room of a small house in Pittsburgh, Pennsylvania. At the same time, Charles N. Miller started a small business manufacturing and selling homemade candy in Boston's Faneuil Hall area, Paul Revere's home until 1800. Then, around the turn of the century, these three New England candy forces joined to build the New England Confectionery Company. It was incorporated with $1 million in capitol and formally named NECCO Sweets.

In 1927, the three firms, now officially NECCO, moved into a newly built manufacturing plant in Boston and created the largest establishment devoted exclusively to the production of confectionery in the United

States. The early NECCO years were good. Workers enjoyed employee benefits. Two and a half tons of NECCO Wafers went to Antarctica with Admiral Byrd on an expedition as nutrition and treats for Eskimo children. To this day, NECCO wafers are the oldest U.S. product continuously manufactured in unchanged form.

In 1938, NECCO was the first candy manufacturer to introduce a molded chocolate bar having four distinctly different centers; it was

Necco advertisement from the 1940s. Necco Wafers are the oldest U.S. product continuously manufactured in an unchanged form.
Dan Goodsell Collection

called "The Candy Box in a Bar." The Sky Bar was first announced to the public with a dramatic airplane sky-writing campaign. However, the war hit and the tide changed for the large candy company. In 1942, NECCO stopped most candy production and turned over a portion of its plant for the manufacture of war materials. Times were lean until V-Day in 1945 when the blackout and curfew in Times Square was lifted.

After three years of darkness, NECCO's Sky Bar advertising sign was relit, celebrating the return of armed forces and candy itself. Straight through the 1990s, NECCO maintained its place in candy history through the manufacturing of creative candy pieces. But it was through buying smaller companies, including Stark Candy Company, the makers of Sweethearts Conversation Heart and the molasses and peanut butter candy Mary Janes; Haviland Chocolates; The Candy House Button Company; Borden Candy Products; and Falcon Candy Company, makers of the peanut butter kiss and salt water taffy, that NECCO grew. Finally in 1999, NECCO acquired the assets of Clark Bar America, makers of the Clark bar, the chocolate-coated peanut butter crunch candy, creating one of the biggest nostalgic American candy forces.

Today NECCO is one of the oldest candy companies in the United States. Comprised of three divisions — NECCO Candy, Stark Candy, and Haviland Candy — they have four manufacturing facilities across the United States. You will recognize many of the company's nostalgic candies: NECCO Wafers, Clark Bar, Sky Bars, Canada Mints, Candy Button Strips, Candy Cupboard Chocolates, Mary Jane, Peanut Butter Kisses, Sweethearts Conversation Hearts, Salt Water Taffy, Slapstix Caramel Pops, Haviland Thin Mints, and Mighty Malts Malted Milk Balls.

D.L. Clark formulated a 5-cent candy bar to supply WW I soldiers. Clark candy bar wrapper from the 1940s.
Courtesy Necco Collection

The company sells four billion NECCO wafers each year and makes eight billion Sweethearts to sell in January and February each year. Both NECCO wafers and Sweethearts are made from the same simple, untouched recipe, containing mostly sugar, of which the company uses almost 20 million pounds per year to make the two candies.

With their lengthy classic candy roster, NECCO is undoubtedly a candy pioneer and a defender of American classic candy.

A vintage Mary Jane standup sign. The original Mary Jane candies were produced in Paul Revere's former house in Boston, Massachusetts.
NECCO Collection

1950s Necco wafer and Sky Bar advertisement.
Beth Kimmerle Collection

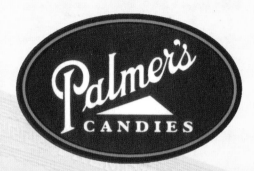

Palmer's Candies

Palmer and Company, originally owned by two sons and their father, E.C. Palmer, started as a fruit whole-saler in 1878. When their fruit business began to expand, the family moved into a natural extension: they began making candy. By 1900, they relocated their thriving business into a four-story building. It was right in the heart of the booming frontier town of Sioux City, Iowa.

Their candy factory was soon making everything from chocolates to gum drops. Palmer produced pieces like the Coconut Ditties, Walnut Grenobles, and Yankee Doodle Popcorn and sold them throughout the bustling Midwest. Their top-notch candy-making facilities had modern equipment like steam boilers and electric generated cold storage. In 1917, with business running smoothly, the company began converting their transportation from horses to thoroughly modern motorized trucks. By the Roaring Twenties, the company was one of the first in town to have a telephone system. Over their phones came in orders for pieces like the Bing Candy Bar. The candy bar was a new way to serve up candy, and Americans were consuming candy bars with fervor.

The Palmer's Bing Candy Bar was special because it came in a variety of fresh flavors supplied by Palmer's own fruit division. However, the top-selling bing cherry flavor outsold the rest and it eventually became the star attraction. The bar became so popular that the company eventually added a "second hump" and created the doubly delicious Twin Bing to meet the growing demand.

Throughout the tough times of the 1930s, the company survived on its quality and value of its candy as well as the fact that it offered an affordable tasty little luxury. Then in 1940, Palmer bought a neighboring candy company along with their equipment: the Soo Candy Company, which specialized in nut roasting. So along with fruits and candy, the Palmers entered into the nut business.

Palmer's Candies prospered throughout the 1950s and 1960s. The firm eventually came to concentrate sole-ly on its candy business. Five generations later, the Palmers still produce the famous Bing Candy Bar along with other confections. Today the company has 140,000 square feet devoted to candy manufacturing, peanut roasting, warehousing, shipping, and offices. With E.C. Palmer's great-great-great-great grandson at the helm of the company and his next-in-line preparing to take over, it seems like Palmer will be doing its "bing" for years to come.

A Palmer wrapper from 1930s.
Palmer Candies Archives

Old 1930s Palmer logo.
Palmer Candies Archives

In 1917, Palmer candy converted its delivery method from horse to motorized vehicles.
Palmer Candies Archives

Palmer candy factory around 1915.
Palmer Candies Archives

The Pearson Candy Company

The Pearson Candy Company was started by a slew of five brothers. P. Edward, John Albert, Oscar F., Waldemar, and C. Fritz Pearson began selling candy in the early 1900s. The Pearson gang soon realized that they could earn money making candy, and in 1912 the 5-cent Nut Goodie Bar made its delicious debut. At that time, candy bars were still a novelty and certainly very original was the idea of mixing ingredients together to form one.

Before long, they were producing candy for other companies like Whitman and Planter's. With the success of their own Nut Goodie, Pearson's grew and soon introduced the Salted Nut Roll. Although it was launched at the height of the Depression, the bar gained popularity because of its delicious taste and great value. The taste was a perfect salty, yet sweet combination of freshly roasted peanuts and caramel over a fluffy nougat center. While other companies tried to mimic the candy taste, Pearson's changed the name to Choo Choo Bar to differentiate it from the others. However, the company still was learning about building a brand and the straightforward Salted Nut Roll name was more successful. The name was changed from Choo Choo back to the simple Salted Nut Roll several years later.

After World War II, the Pearson brothers decided to drop their distribution business entirely to concentrate on candy manufacturing. While family members came and went, business went on very successfully. In 1951, Pearson's purchased the Trudeau Candy Company of St. Paul, Minnesota, known for the famed Mint Pattie and the Seven Up bar. The Seven Up candy bar was comprised of seven chocolate sections that contained different flavors. The wrapper read, "7 Delicious Varieties In One Bar." Butterscotch Caramel, Cherry Cream, Fudge, Orange Jelly, Nougat, Coconut and Butter Cream, and Brazil Nut were just a few of the delicious centers. Flavors changed based on availability of the commodity and popularity of flavors. The bar was phased out entirely in 1979 when dark chocolate covered segments of mint, nougat, butterscotch, fudge, coconut, buttercream, and caramel. Sadly, the Seven Up bar was too time-consuming and expensive to make. Today, it is the fondly remembered as one of the extinct super-star bars.

In 1959, when Pearson's was celebrating its 50th anniversary, the company moved from downtown St. Paul to a new manufacturing plant at its current address. While other candy companies were leaving the area or closing up shop, Pearson's continued to make the fresh candy the firm had become famous for. It continued to purchase companies like Milwaukee-based Sperry Candy in 1962. Sperry Candy Company originally created the Chicken Dinner and the Club Sandwich Bar. Five years later, Sperry was sold to Winona's Schuler Chocolate Factory.

After much candy coming and going, the Pearson family decided to sell their business in 1968. Sadly, Pearson's was again sold off ten years later to a company that almost shattered the Pearson brands. By changing recipes and altering the recognizable packaging, the famous bars lost loyal customers. Even St. Paul area fans of Pearson's candies had trouble finding their favorite products in stores.

Then in 1985, two loyal Pearson employees purchased Pearson's Candy Company. Their goal was to give the Pearson brand the attention it so richly deserved and return the Pearson products to the quality that had made them famous. The Nut Goodie's original wrapper and recipe returned, as did loyal customers.

Today, the Salted Nut Roll, Nut Goodie, and Pearson's Mint Patties continue. In 1998, Pearson's acquired the Bun Bar trademark from Clark Bar America. The Bun brand, which was first manufactured in the early 1900s, has a similar history to Pearson's Nut Goodie and fit nicely in the family of Pearson favorites. Pearson's is celebrating over 90 years of St. Paul candy making, and the popularity of its candy shows no sign of abating.

Philadelphia Gum Company

Dr. Edward P. Fenimore, Sr., knew about gum. He had been a professor of chemical engineering at University of Pennsylvania before taking a job as vice-president of the Bowman Gum Company. Bowman Gum was famous for their big two inches of bubble gum called Blony and was the first gum maker to put a collectible card inside their gum packs. Edward P. Fenimore not only understood gum formulations, he was an astute businessman who went on to open his own gum company.

1946 was a tough year to start a gum business. The war had just ended and necessary gum-making ingredients like sugar were still rationed. Equipment for manufacturing was also scarce due to the war. Most machinery efforts were put towards making planes and other war gear. The government strictly for wartime use allocated steel and other metals. With minimal ingredients and a few salvaged machines Ed Fenimore's startup business was opened.

The effort was worth it. Bubble gum was in enormous demand as it was virtually cut off during the war years; the nominal gum that was produced went directly to the armed forces. When around-the-clock production of Fenimore's Super Bubble began, the gum sold as fast as it was made. As supplies became widely available, business grew and soon many others entered the gum game.

By the late 1940s, Philadelphia Chewing Gum was producing its popular twist-wrapped Swell gum for a penny but needed a gum to differentiate itself in the sticky-pink saturated market. With more competition, the gum company determined it would need a bigger piece that could sell for more than a penny. How would the company make something novel enough that would entice kids to spend five times the going gum rate? Ed P. Fenimore puffed on his imported cigar and thought about it.

A brown colored cigar-shaped gum complete with a gold embossed band named El Bubble was born. It was the first post-war gum to sell for five cents and was soon known nationwide, carried by all 2,500 Woolworth stores. By 1954, the company's popular Magic Color gum cigarettes became the first ten-cent bubble gum pack on the market. Philadelphia's gum cigars and cigarettes were both smokin' hits.

Swell Presidential Favorites bubble gum cigars have been smokin' since the 1960s.
Philadelphia Gum Collection

Edward L. Fenimore, Jr., who had worked in the Bowman Gum Factory when he was in college, also knew the gum business. He took over in 1955 and grew Philadelphia Chewing Gum literally by expanding the facility and by entering into new business. Between 1960 and 1975, James Bond, Dark Shadows, and Marvel Comics were a few of the trading cards produced by Philadelphia Gum. They became hot sellers for collecting kids.

In 1975, just as Edward's sons entered into the world of gum, the company got an important contract to manufacture an experimental gum for Life Savers. The gum was to be the first soft bubble gum, and this tender pink square blew bigger bubbles than anyone had ever seen. The gum that swept the market was called Bubble Yum.

With their classics like Swell and El Bubble cigars along with new favorites like Cry Baby extra sour, Philadelphia Chewing Gum continues their long history of innovation in bubble gum. Edward L. Fenimore remains the president of Philadelphia Chewing Gum and chairman of the National Association of Chewing Gum Manufacturers. Today, with his sons, Edward P. and Richard, the company is in its third generation as a family-owned and operated business. Together, as a family, the Fenimores continue to make bubbles happen.

Swell gum advertisement, 1950s.

Sifers Candy Company

The Sifers have been making candy since 1903. Samuel Mitchell Sifers had a small production of penny candy and chocolates. He also produced some of the original 5-cent candy bars in the Midwest. His little candy factory located in Iola, Kansas, made wonderfully named candy bars like Old King Tut, Subway Sadie, Fumbles, Snow Cup, and the KC Bar.

By the 1920s, the busy company was located in a larger factory in Kansas City. It made a variety of candy bars and specialized in fresh marshmallow candies. The wonderful, handmade, fluffy marshmallow contained delicious real vanilla extract. The pricey vanilla had great flavor but also contained a large amount of alcohol. According to the Sifers, Tommy, their candy maker, took a few nips of the vanilla while preparing a batch of fresh marshmallow. In turn, he "overserved" the batch, pouring in too much vanilla. The result was a marshmallow that was delicious but would not fluff up. Instead of firming up after cooling, the marshmallow remained runny. The company was always eager to try new creations and did not let the liquid marshmallow goop go to waste. They poured the runny marshmallow mix into dark chocolate candy cups. The result was a messy yet very tasty original new candy. The "intoxicating" Valomilk was invented, quite by accident.

They called it the Valomilk Dip: V for real vanilla extract, ALO from marshmallow, MILK to describe its creamy insides and DIP because it was hand-dipped or handmade. "The Original Flowing Center Candy Cup" was the tag line that described the innovative candy to early experimenters.

The Valomilk Dip gained a loyal following throughout the Midwest. The company continued to flourish, while new family members joined in making candy. Valiantly dedicated to their candy customers, the Sifers continued to make their candy through wars and recessions. During WWII, when vital candy ingredients were rationed, the company had someone fly around the country in an open cockpit plane, searching for necessary ingredients to make Valomilks. They would do what it took to get their candy to their adoring public.

Sifers' Valomilk Candy Company was sold to Hoffman Candy Company in 1970. Hoffman, a longtime candy company, knew a good thing when it saw it. They attempted to build a huge candy corporation comprised of smaller regional candy makers. Russ Sifers joined the candy conglomerate as a fourth generation candy maker. However, the Sifers' factory shut down in 1981 after merger difficulties and business differences. After more than 50 years of production, the Valomilk was tragically no longer available on store shelves.

Years later, Russ discovered his great-grandfather's original copper candy kettles while clearing out his old factory. Candy making was clearly in his blood, and Russ decided it was time to dip again. Helped by his family and friends, Russ put the historic candy factory back together. By 1987, Valomilks had made a triumphant rebirth and returned to Midwestern stores. Dave Sifers, Russ' son, is the fifth generation to carry on the Valomilk tradition, while a sixth generation is in training.

Valomilks are made the old-fashioned way, using Tommy's recipe along with much of the original equipment. The candy is even wrapped much like it was originally. They are made one batch at a time, resulting in an fresh quality you can taste. If you have the opportunity to try the chocolate cup with the flowing center, do. You'll taste Sifers pride in every delicious bite.

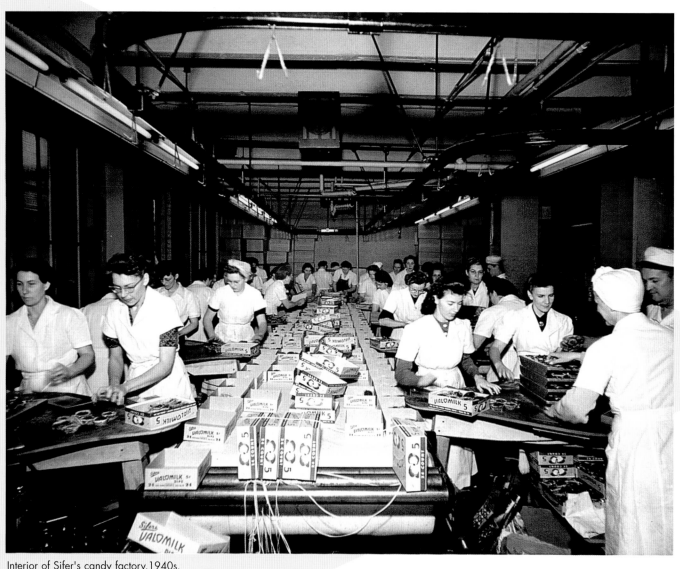

Interior of Sifer's candy factory, 1940s.
The women are dipping the vanilla
marshmallow center into chocolate.
Sifers Collection

1960s Valomilk wrapper.
Beth Kimmerle Collection

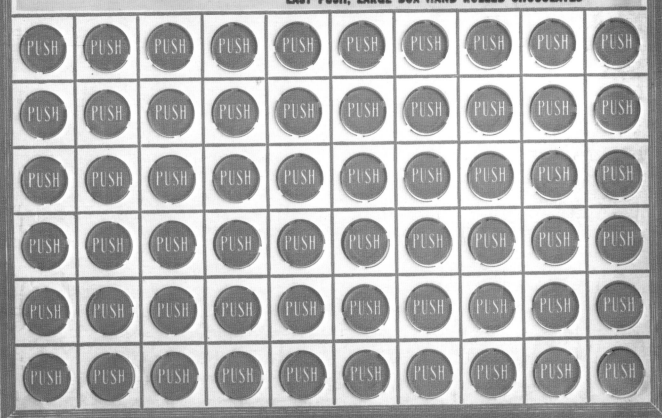

Candy punchcards promoted candy consumption through glorified gambling–fun!

Michael Rosenberg Collection

Spangler Candy Company

Spangler signature products include familiar names like Dum Dum Pops, Saf-T-Pops, Astro Pops, Spangler Candy Canes, and Spangler Circus Peanuts. Dum Dums and Saf-T-Pops are the yummy little kiddie lollipops associated with bank visits and treat bowls. Spangler has manufactured many great candies in their 100-year history. Over the years they have also made soda pop, cough drops, taffy, and marshmallow topping.

The company started back in 1906 when Arthur Spangler acquired Gold Leaf Baking Powder for $406 from a local sheriff's sale and moved the operation to his hometown of Bryan, Ohio. There, he changed the name to Spangler Manufacturing Co. and continued manufacturing and distributing baking supplies, including baking powder, baking soda, spices, and candy flavorings. Arthur's mother, Clara, began using her son's supplies to make salted and candied peanuts from a small kettle in her home.

At the request of Arthur's brother, Ernest, a candy salesman in nearby Toledo, he added other candy items to his product line and in 1911 acquired the rights to a popular coconut item. The Spangler brothers hired the man who created the product, moved him to Bryan, and introduced the Spangler Cocoanut Ball — Spangler's first candy brand. The Cocoanut Ball was manufactured with real coconuts that were hand-cracked with hatchets by a crew that was paid $1.50 per day for their labor. At its peak, the popular Cocoanut Ball piece was sold to most Woolworth's across the states.

With business booming, a third brother, Omar, joined the firm in 1914. Omar's specialty was accounting. Omar brought much needed mechanical and bookkeeping knowledge to the team. Spangler was manufacturing a range of confections and sweets like Creme Peanut Clusters, Cocoanut Balls, Bryan Drops, hand-dipped chocolates, chocolate bars, ice cream cones, soda pop, and cough drops.

In 1920, a fourth brother, Truman, joined the company as a salesman. By that time, all products manufactured at the company were candy, so the name was changed from Spangler Manufacturing Company to Spangler Candy Company. Together the brothers grew the business by trying and retiring various candy products. By 1925, over 60 items kept the brothers in business. The best-sellers included Cherry Balls, Hickok Honeycomb Chocolate, and Marshmallow Topping.

Huge successes came in the 1950s with the purchase of Dum Dum Pops and A-Z Christmas Candy Canes of Detroit, Michigan. The famous Saf-T-Pops, which rounded out the lollipop line-up, was purchased from Curtiss Candy Co. of Chicago, Illinois, in 1978.

Today, Spangler is still run by descendants of the original brothers. The chairman of Spangler Candy is C. Gregory Spangler, grandson of founder Ernest Spangler. The president and CEO is Dean L. Spangler, grandson of founder Omar Spangler. Spangler is still located in Bryan, Ohio, a town of about 10,000. They are set up in a state-of-the-art manufacturing facility, covering 500,000 square feet. Currently, the company manufactures about seven million Dum Dum lollipops, one million Saf-T-Pops, and about 2.5 million candy canes every day.

1953

Dum Dum Pops were invented by Akron Candy in 1924.

1957

The banana-flavored circus peanut is truly one of the most controversial candies ever. Questions surrounding the candy include: Why orange colored? Why banana flavored? Why circus named?

Squirrel Brand Salted Nut Company

Makers of the famous Squirrel Nut Zipper, the Squirrel Brand Company's origins go back to 1892 when the company was started as the Austin T. Merrill Company in Massachusetts. The Squirrel Brand Salted Nut Company was incorporated in 1899 and shortly after was sold to new owners, including two veteran employees, Perley G. Gerrish and Fred S. Green. In the hands of the new owners, the nut business grew quickly and moved in 1903 to new quarters in Cambridge, Massachusetts.

By 1911, they were roasting and salting over a million pounds of peanuts a year. In addition, substantial quantities of pecans, walnuts, cashews, and almonds were produced. Perley Gerrish introduced his hit peanut bar in 1905 by handing out samples to schoolchildren along his candy and nut delivery route. His popular nut caramel piece followed in 1911. A growing business and increasing automation required another move in 1915 to a new and bigger building. A four-story structure on Boardman Street in Cambridge was to be the home of Squirrel Brand until 1999. This is the same building that inspired the popular 1990s music talents to name their retro band the Squirrel Nut Zippers.

Throughout the 1920s, 1930s, and 1940s, Squirrel Brand expanded its offerings to include such candy items as Butter Chews, Nut Twins, Nut Chews, Nut Yippee, Butta Babies, Peanut Butter Kisses, and Cocoanut Zippers along with flavored and saltwater taffy.

During Prohibition, a Vermont man was talked down from a tree during a "crazy" episode. He later blamed his condition on some local hooch he referred to as "that dang nut zipper." Around the same time, the famous vanilla caramel nut taffy, the Squirrel Nut Zipper, was invented. A new crazy candy concoction, it was named after this illegal drink.

By the 1940s, most Squirrel Nut products were being shipped and distributed nationwide. Even the U.S. Navy and Army were supplied with the famous candy and nut products. Squirrel Brand peanuts went on expeditions to the South Pole with Admiral Byrd. Innovation in marketing continued with radio advertising in 1929. In 1937, Squirrel Brand continued its appeal to children by offering a free pencil imprinted with the child's name in return for sending four empty bags of Squirrel Brand peanuts. Between 1937 and 1953, over 350,000 personalized pencils were shipped out. This popular nutty pencil promotion lasted into the 1970s.

The management and candy has remained relatively consistent at Squirrel Brand for many years. Fred Green died in 1919 and Perley Gerrish assumed full control until his death in 1939. Hollis G. Gerrish took over from his father as president until his death at age 91 in 1997. Hollis wanted the business to stay in the hands of small producers, and the outfit was sold to a Squirrel Brand supplier, Southern Style Nuts, Inc., in 1999.

Squirrel Brand Caramels, 1930.
Squirrel Brand Collection

Squirrel Brand Peanuts, 1930.
Squirrel Brand Collection

Squirrel Brand Nut Chews, 1940.
Squirrel Brand Collection

Standard Candy Company

In 1901, Howell Campbell, a southern candy maker, founded Standard Candy Company in Nashville, Tennessee. Originally located on First Avenue in downtown Nashville, Campbell, a 19-year-old, eager entrepreneur, had big dreams for his new candy company. Campbell's business, started from his home kitchen, soon grew into a flourishing family enterprise known throughout the region for its delicious assortment of high-quality confections. The first products sold by Campbell were hard candies and chocolates. His most well-known candy, the Goo Goo Cluster, was a completely new and revolutionary candy invention made as a fluke while Campbell was testing ingredients in his small candy kitchen.

In 1912, Campbell's delicious ingredient accident developed into "America's 1st Combination Candy Bar." He was the very first confectioner to make a candy bar with multiple ingredients and not simply solid milk chocolate. He made the unique Goo Goo Clusters by combining peanuts, caramel, marshmallow, and milk chocolate into a deliciously round cluster. Goo Goos were originally sold unwrapped in big glass candy display jars. People love Campbell's delicious, creative concoction, and the popular Goo Goos quickly became the company's best-selling product.

There are quite a few stories about how the uniquely round-shaped Goo Goo Cluster got its name. Some say the origins are directly related to the Grand Ole Opry, but the actual story, the company says, is a little different. Apparently, Campbell rode a streetcar to work every day. Soon after he developed his delicious new confection, word spread quickly about the tasty treat. People didn't know how to ask for the confectionery delight. Campbell was extremely excited that his newest concoction was the talk of the town, but even he was baffled as to what to call his candy piece. One day while on the streetcar, Campbell was discussing his dilemma with a fellow passenger. The lady, a schoolteacher, remarked that the unique candy bar was "so good, people will ask for it from birth!" Thinking about what the woman said, Campbell recalled the first sounds his newborn son made. Goo Goo Clusters were officially named.

In the 1920s and 1930s, to promote his new popular Goo Goo Cluster candy bars, Campbell advertised them as "A Nourishing Lunch For a Nickel!" During the Depression, Goo Goos were a great value for the many people who didn't have much money. In addition, urban workers were not able to go home for lunch; a big industrial shift had taken place. Lunch became something eaten on the run. Lunch also needed to be inexpensive. The Goo Goo, rich in flavor, was indeed an inexpensive solution for hungry workers looking for a tasty treat.

Since Standard Candy was founded, the company has changed hands twice, but not much else has changed. Mr. Campbell, Jr., took over the company's operation from his father, and eventually the Campbell family sold the company to other confectioners. In the 1970s, two Nashville businessmen purchased Standard Candy and relocated the plant to its present location in Tennessee. In 1982, the Spradley family acquired the candy company. In 1985, the Spradleys purchased the Stuckey's candy plant in Eastman, Georgia. The Spradley focus was to build sales by distributing products nationally, not just regionally. Throughout the rest of the 1980s and 1990s, distribution of the Goo Goo began to grow into all of the southeastern states. Now, the Goo Goo can be found from Florida to California, allowing new candy eaters, as well as those who remember them from their southern childhood, to enjoy them.

Standard Candy's formula for success has been as simple and straightforward as the day the company was founded in 1901; the company focuses on quality candy and tradition. The company now manufactures close to 75,000 Goo Goo pieces a day. Some new flavors have been added, and the candy packaging has been slightly updated, but for the most part, this nostalgic favorite remains the same as when it was made by mistake some 90 years ago.

Early Goo Goo display box.
Standard collection

Standard collection

Goo Goo clusters have been popular since 1912 when they were invented. They were some of the very first marketed "combination" candy bars — with nuts, chocolate, and caramel.
Standard collection

Goo Goo Clusters have been a Nashville favorite — regularly featured at the Grand Ole Opry.
Standard collection.

Want a sweet chew?
Try a *GooGoo* !

GooGoo®
Cluster
NET WT 1-3/4 OZS.

GooGoo® Cluster
NET WT 1-3/4 OZS.

GooGoo®

The South's favorite candy for 68 years.
Get one at the Concession Stand.
Manufactured by Standard Candy Co., Nashville, Tennessee

Goo Goo Clusters were named for the sounds a baby makes. "So good, people will ask for it from birth."
Standard collection.

Sweets Company of America

Every candy fan knows and loves a Tootsie Roll. Chewy, cocoa-flavored, and shaped like a roll, it is available in a variety of different sizes. With a recipe unchanged, they have been around for more than 100 years. Amazingly, Tootsie Rolls still sell for a penny.

In 1896, Leo Hirschfield, an Austrian immigrant, made a chocolate candy that was similar to taffy, somewhat like fudge, and a close relative to caramel. The concoction was one that Leo adapted from an old family recipe. He named it for his daughter, Clara. Her nickname was "Tootsie." Soon, it became the first wrapped penny candy. Because it was long lasting, as well as wrapped for freshness, it could be sold far and wide — and it was. The candy grew so popular that by 1922, the Sweets Company of America went public and was officially listed on the New York Stock Exchange.

With a naturally long shelf life, nothing much can affect a Tootsie Roll. They are deliciously invincible. In fact, during World War II, the Tootsie Roll was one of a handful of candies allowed to remain in production. The Sweets Company supplied the U.S. Army with their famous candy that could last under the harsh war conditions. Tootsie Rolls were produced as a part of G.I. rations and loved by the troops. Many soldiers came home with stories about how the magic little candy helped keep their spirits up.

In 1931, a Tootsie Roll got dipped in hard candy, found a home on a paper stick, and the Tootsie Pop was made. "How many licks does it take to get to the Tootsie Roll center of a Tootsie Pop?" This was the question that a curious young boy asked a wise and bespectacled Owl on national TV. The owl's answer was three, after two licks he bit through to the Tootsie Roll. In the 1970s, we all tried to find out too, again and again, moving through tons of lollipops — testing, licking, and impatiently biting.

Along with their famous original Tootsie Roll and Tootsie Pops, the company now produces many other nostalgic favorites, including Sugar Babies, Charms, Mason Dots, Junior Mints, and the taffy Charleston Chew. Charms, Inc., makers of Charms and Blow Pops, is now owned by Tootsie, which purchased it in 1988.

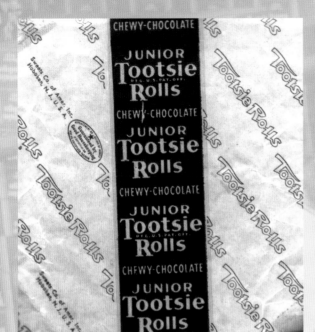

1940s Tootsie Roll "midgie" wrapper.
Beth Kimmerle Collection

Sugar Babies, originally developed by Welch's Candy, were named for a song titled, "Let Me Be Your Sugar Baby."
Dan Goodsell Collection

Charms hard candy squares and lollipop joined Tootsie Rolls in 1988.
Dan Goodsell Collection

Charms had been around since 1917, making a great, square-shaped, fruity hard candy. Their famous hard candy now comes on a stick in a bright wrapper decorated with dots — it's a Charms Pop. When the candy contains a secret stash of gum, you've got a Blow Pop. The purchase of Charms has made Tootsie the largest lollipop manufacturer in the world, making 20 million pieces a day!

Mason Dots, Black Crows, Sugar Babies, and Junior Mints are all theater favorites and came to Tootsie Roll under separate acquisitions. In 1972, the Tootsie Company bought Mason and gained the famously sticky Mason Dots and Black Crows. Black Crows were originally developed with the name Black Rose. However, when the name was given to the printer who was printing the early wrappers, he heard the name as Black Crows.

In 1993, Tootsie purchased Warner-Lambert's great candy brands, bringing Junior Mints, Sugar Daddy, Sugar Babies, and Charleston Chews to their Tootsie Roll, candy-making home. A company called Welch's launched the Junior Mint in 1949. Brothers Robert and James ran it. Robert Welch named the minty candy after his favorite Broadway stage performance, Junior Miss. With the mint center and the light coat of chocolate, he developed a perfect, bite-size piece specifically for shows and theater. Its inventor, Robert Welch, then a Cambridge, Massachusetts, chocolate salesman, introduced the Sugar Daddy in 1926. The caramel candy was first called the Papa Sucker but was changed to the substantially more charming Sugar Daddy in 1932. Sugar Babies were born shortly following their Daddy's arrival and were named after a song, "Let Me Be Your Sugar Baby." Charleston Chews were named for the Roaring Twenties dance craze, the Charleston. Along with the well-loved vanilla and chocolate, the chocolate-coated taffy swings away in strawberry, too. The candy still delights today.

Husband-and-wife team, Ellen and Melvin Gordon, now run Tootsie Roll Industries. Ellen started her career at Tootsie testing candy flavors. Then one summer, she took a job in the company advertising department as a model. An ad with the perky Gordon was featured in *Life* magazine in 1950. Ellen Gordon's family has been involved with the company since the start. Her great grandfather was a paper supplier to Leo Hirschfield. Her family became majority shareholders in the late 1930s. Ellen Gordon was named president of Tootsie Roll Industries, Inc., in 1978. She was the second woman to be elected president of a company listed on the New York Stock Exchange. Today, Ellen doesn't seem much different than the Ellen from the *Life* magazine ad. The company has added many different candies and technologies to their line-up, but she's still got that youthful spirit. Now, along with their other candies, the company produces over 60 million Tootsie Rolls a day. And talk about Tootsie Roll being long lasting — Tootsie Roll even outlasted the venerable *Life* magazine. Now, that's a piece of candy!

Junior Mints are now known as the candy with "powers from above" from their cameo role on *Seinfeld*.
Dan Goodsell Collection.

Matches were a perfect advertising place for candy as they were picked up at counters where candy was sold.
Beth Kimmerle Collection.

Vintage Charms Blow Pop wrappers.
Dan Goodsell Collection

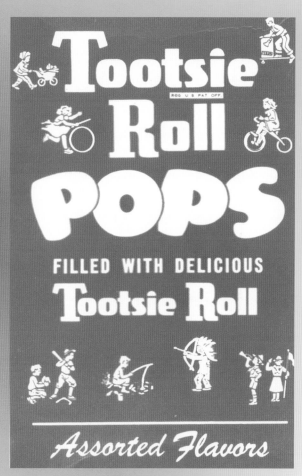

Tootsie Roll now produces 20 Million Tootsie Pops per day!
Dan Goodsell Collection

Bazooka Joe Comic, circa 1950.
Joe's eyepatch mimicked the "Hathaway Man"
– ad executive David Ogilvy's famed and
distinctive shirt salesman.
Dan Goodsell Collection

Topps Gum

The Brooklyn-based Shorin brothers got into gum in 1938, ten years after it was invented. They started with a penny-candy product simply called Topps Gum. They would later become famous for their highly collectible baseball cards and Bazooka brand bubble gum. "Don't talk, chum; chew Topps gum." This was their advertising slogan that helped sell gum during WWII.

After the war, the simple Topps Gum slowly evolved into Bazooka bubble gum. Fleer Gum was the first to wrap a comic around their pink gum. Fleer developed a character called Pud who graced comics with the stories of his adventures with pal, Rocky Roller. However, Topps comics starred a young boy who was not only funny and had a gang of friends, he wore an eye patch for dramatic effect. Bazooka Joe was created and his comics began to blanket gum in 1953. About 700 comic strips later, Joe sports a slightly updated style but doesn't look or act his 50 years.

Bazooka Gum was named for a goofy musical instrument made from two gas pipes and a funnel, played by comedian Bob Burns in the 1930s. Kids redeemed their collected Bazooka comics for exotic sounding prizes. Super spy telescopes, Flexy Racers, shoe-strapping roller skates, and real flying kites were just some of the treats a chewing habit could bring.

Today Bazooka, with its flag-colored wrapper, is an icon of America. Bazooka comics are still collected and their premiums still redeemed today. Topps claims that a psychological study of tastes and smells that evoke memories found that one of the most frequently identified products was our beloved Bazooka bubble gum.

Trading cards had been packaged with cigarettes since 1885. They were first paired with gum in the 1930s, and Topps offered its first cards in 1950. They featured TV's favorite cowboy, Hopalong Cassidy, "Bring 'em Back Alive" African Safari cards, and All-American football cards.

Topps matches, circa 1940.
Beth Kimmerle Collection.

In 1951, baseball game cards were introduced. However, a Topps employee, baseball fan, and marketing mastermind, Sy Berger, brought them to a different level later with the inclusion of player details, records, and statistics. He, in effect, developed the modern baseball card. Mickey Mantle and Willie Mays were rookies in 1952, and today their cards are worth over $8000 each. The original oil painting commissioned for the Mantle card sold in 1989 for over $120,000. Collectors continue to cherish the 1952 Topps baseball cards.

By 1956, Topps had signed most major league baseball players to their cards. That year, Topps purchased the Bowman Company, makers of the famous Blony gum. Blony was said to produce bubbles "twice as large as any other." Bowman often touted the Blony gum value — a mere penny for a huge piece. But more importantly, Bowman was the first gum maker to insert a collectible card in their package. Initially, their small-sized cards depicted images of cowboys and Indians and then later, American war heroes. With the purchase of Bowman, Topps became a first string player in cards.

Soon, their collectible cards became more popular than the gum they were packaged with. Topps has created a card for every sport fan with basketball, football, and hockey players smiling away on cardboard. Culture fans have also scored with sets developed for Star Wars, Michael Jackson, and the Kennedy family. For those interested in haute culture, Topps offered Wacky Packages and Garbage Pail Kids. Cards are now displayed in art museums and the Baseball Hall of Fame. They bring top dollar at auctions and card shows.

The international Topps remains a huge player in gum and confectionery with their classic Bazooka, highly collectible cards, and newer favorites, Ring Pops, Push Pops, Baby Bottle Pops, and Juice Bar Bubble Gum. Today, Topps remains at the tippy-top of their gum game.

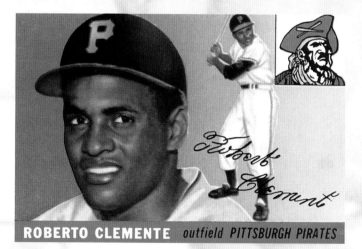

1955 Roberto Clemente baseball card.
Topps Collection.

One half billion pieces of Bazooka are sold each year.
One gum collector displays his share.
Jeff Nelson Collection

Juicy Fruit is the oldest brand
in the Wrigley family.
Courtesy Wrigley

Wrigley

Wrigley produced the same three favors of gum for 59 years. The same three flavors, at five cents a pack, made a man rich enough to open a baseball field in a major city, buy an island off the coast of California, and build a massive terra cotta office building — one of the first skyscrapers of its kind. That man was William Wrigley, Jr. He started as a Chicago-area salesman, selling his father's scouring soap. As the soap became less interesting to his customers than the product bonus he was giving away as incentive, he quickly switched gears.

Wrigley first went to market with gums called Vassar and Lotta. In 1902, he offered simple flavors like vanilla, orange, and peach. But soon he was exclusively producing the now internationally known Juicy Fruit and Spearmint.

By 1910, Wrigley's Spearmint was the top-selling gum in North America. His third hit, Double Mint, was introduced in 1914 and started an empire. The Wrigley Building, a beautifully ornate skyscraper on Chicago's magnificent mile, has become a city landmark. Its gleaming white tile-adorned facade is lit up at night by powerful lights that line the Chicago River. Created in the 1930s, the distinctive building is featured in architecture books and proudly stands in many movies.

Wrigley purchased lush Catalina Island in the early 1900s for $2 million. On the enchanted property, he built a resort complete with a lavish dance hall as well as a bird aviary that became home to thousands of exotic birds. The island sits 26 miles across the sea and is a magical nature wonderland to this day. The Wrigley name is still connected to Wrigley Field, home of the Chicago Cubs. The baseball team was sold, but Wrigley's name is still on the classic field. The baseball field only recently adopted lights. Philip K. Wrigley, son of the founder and president of the company from 1925-1961, resisted the lights, beating a lawsuit brought by minority stockholders who wanted the night games to generate revenue. He felt that a lit ballpark, located in a family neighborhood, would disrupt too many lives.

Merits your lasting esteem because of its long-lasting flavor

Sealed Tight—Kept Right

Enjoy Delicious Wrigley's Chewing Gum Daily ... Millions Do. Chewing these delightful treats aids digestion — helps sweeten your breath — helps brighten your teeth

See how quickly this mild, real-mint flavor refreshes your taste. Wherever you are, chewing delicious Doublemint Gum adds fun to everything you do. Inexpensive ... good and good for you. Enjoy daily.

Treat yourself to lively, he-man flavor every day. Full of wholesome chewing fun, Wrigley's Spearmint is popular with young and old. Costs little ... great to enjoy. The Flavor Lasts.

Here's a real bargain in pleasure. Satisfying, swell-tasting "Juicy Fruit" offers you smooth chewing and lots of refreshing, long-lasting flavor. Ideal between meals. An American favorite for nearly 50 years.

Your friendly local merchant has a large display of Wrigley Brands of Chewing Gum on his counter for your convenience

William Wrigley, Jr. was a firm believer in advertising. This mailed gum give-away went to early telephone service subscribers.

By 1933, many of Wrigley's ads were airbrushed by Otis Shepard. His design style is iconic and highly regarded in commercial arts.
Courtesy Wrigley.

Wrigley delivers, 1901.
Courtesy Wrigley.

(Background image: Wrigley building, 1920s.)

While William Wrigley, Jr., was considered quite flamboyant with his assets, he was also a respected employer. He was fair to workers, offering them life insurance and annual wage guarantees. At the factories, laundry and manicures were made available to his busy workers. He was also partly responsible for the current work week structure. He was the first employer in the United States to grant a two-day weekend.

William Wrigley, Jr., was a fan of advertising, and the company remains a top Madison Avenue client today. Due to his days as a salesman on the road, Wrigley was well aware of the power of advertising and free samples. When Alexander Bell's new invention, the telephone, was gaining popularity, Wrigley obtained a list of all subscribers in the United States and sent them a free pack of Spearmint gum. He always believed that a message should be simple, unobtrusive, and to the point. His motto was tell 'em quick and tell 'em often, resulting in ads that were straightforward with minimal copy. His famous Doublemint Twins showed their lovely faces in the 1930s. Today, many twin sets have been part of the longest advertising campaign ever developed in America.

Wrigley was an innovator in packaging and invented the foil wrapper that keeps sticks fresh and full of flavor. The extra paper became a part of the gum experience, allowing chewers a receptacle to discard sticky gum. Wrigley was also the first to put cellophane around an entire pack to shield against moisture and to ensure that his product arrived safely on store shelves. His cellophane introduction, so novel in 1932, required instructions to be printed on the label. The directions read, "To open unwind red tape."

The company, always concerned with quality, discontinued their product when, during World War II, sugar and other ingredients were rationed. The company felt it could not make a decent product and ceased prodcution instead of offering a limited supply to only a handful. The company, while waiting to get back to business, introduced an ad campaign reminding America to "Remember This Wrapper," depicting a lonely, empty spearmint wrapper without gum.

Wrigley has remained successful due to a focus on a fine and simple product. Early on, Wrigley concentrated on a few brands and refused to produce trendy flavors and for years wouldn't touch trendy bubble gum. When competitors like Fleer and Bazooka were well entrenched in a blowable gum, the Wrigley Company finally decided to venture into bubble gum and set up a separate business to do so. That business is called Amurol and now produces top toy/gum pieces like Bubble Tape and Big League Chew. It wasn't until 1975 that Wrigley introduced Big Red, a cinnamon-flavored gum, perhaps created to give the popular Dentyne, launched in 1930, a run for its money. It may have taken a while to get the product to market, but by 1987 the gum was the top-selling cinnamon-flavored piece in the mouths of America.

The next products to hit shelves were Extra sugar-free gum and the super-cool Winterfresh. But even with these new introductions, Wrigley's product rarely changes. Once in a while, there is a slight packaging boost. The gum, however, remains the same size and shape. Like many things that William Wrigley, Jr., built and created, the gum remains simply magical. William Wrigley, Jr., once said, "Nothing great was ever achieved without enthusiasm." Enthusiasm for Wrigley's gum continues.

To the Children of the World— "from 6 to 60"

in the hope that it will serve to pass many a happy hour and point a way to much beneficial pleasure at small cost in **WRIGLEY'S** this book is dedicated.

Wm. Wrigley Jr. Co.
CHICAGO
NEW YORK
TORONTO
LONDON, ENG.
PARIS   MELBOURNE

For additional copies of this booklet address
WM. WRIGLEY JR. CO., 1200 Kesner Bldg.
CHICAGO

"GOOD FRIENDS, WE GREET YOU!"

"PLEASED TO MEET YOU!"

The spear or arrow from Wrigley's spearmint gum was the star of the company's famous cartoon series in the 1920s and 1930s.
Courtesy Wrigley .

1905

1924

1932

1941

1957

1989

Oh mommy jus' the kind I like !

163

INTRODUCTION TO CANDY MAKING

A great way to customize your own sweet favorites, making candy at home can be really entertaining. Making candy takes some patience, some basic equipment, and a few pointers.

Be sure to read recipes thoroughly before starting for an understanding of precisely what needs to take place from beginning to end. Because temperature plays a critical role in candy making, procedures often occur rapidly before mixes cool or overheat. Stirring mixes can cause sugars to re-crystallize. Only stir mixes when instructed and with a wooden spoon, not metal. Kitchen surfaces and utensils need to be very clean and dry before starting. Foreign elements, even a drop of water, can alter tastes and textures. For any candy making, thermometers are a must.

Most candy recipes begin by combining sugars and water. Before the use of thermometers, candy makers tested temperatures by dipping their mixtures into a cold water bath to distinguish the results. The cold water test is still referred to in recipes. It takes a keen and trained eye to use this method. I often use both a thermometer and cold water to see the exact reaction and to insure that my thermometer is on target.

To test with cold water, prepare a small bowl with one cup of cold water. When temperature is at desired level, drop one teaspoon of your mix into to the bowl. When candy recipes refer to ball stages, they mean the hardness of sugar when it is rolled into a ball between your fingers. Mixtures heated to a lower temperature 235-240F or soft-ball stage, create candies like fondants and fudges. Recipes that call for longer cooking, 245-250F or firm-ball stage, make candies in the caramel family. 250-265F, hard-ball stage, is the heating level for rock candies.

As cooking temperatures rise, sugar hardens and liquid cooks off. Crack stages are recognizable through the sugar brittleness. Soft-crack, heating between 270-290F, creates toffees and taffies. Hard-cracked sugar heats at 300-310F and will form lollipops and hard candies. Cooked caramelized sugar, turning brown at 320-338F, is the temperature for producing pralines and candied nuts.

Tempering chocolate involves heating and then cooling chocolate. The process stabilizes it, keeping the cocoa butter from separating from the chocolate. It is best to use a double boiler to prevent overheating and scorching. Precisely tempered chocolate will have an even, smooth, shiny surface. Tempered chocolate will provide a perfect coating for your dipped fruits, handmade truffles, caramels, and marshmallows.

A successful batch of taffy or truffles is gratifying. In time, you can explore new tastes by varying ingredients and flavorings. New looks can be achieved by using candy molds and food colors. I have made my own and been exposed to large-scale candy making for years. To sharpen my skills in the craft, I took a course at the Institute of Culinary Education, founded by Peter Kump in New York. Official training has saved lots of nougat from becoming taffy.

If you can't find a local course, team up with someone who makes candy. In most communities, there is a candy maven in the mix. Just ask your friends where they get the delicious holiday fudge and handmade caramels.

Perhaps home candy making will lead to a small confection business or maybe even the next big candy bar. Many American candy makers started at home. Let their stories inspire.

CHAPTER 7

Candy-making equipment list:

2 Thermometers
Ca^ndy and chocolate
Candy molds and vegetable oil spray for molds
Dipping tool for chocolate coating
Double boiler and several sizes of heavy gauge pans for even cooking
Pastry brushes for eliminating crystals on pans and brushing molds
Scissors
Wax and parchment papers
Marble or other cold, non-stick, flat work surface

Recipes

Peanut Brittle

*This caramelized sugar treat with nestled nuts is heavenly. Substitute
almonds for peanuts for another delight: almond brittle.*

- **2 tablespoons unsalted butter, room temperature**
- **1 cup granulated sugar**
- **1/2 cup light corn syrup**
- **1/2 cup cold water**
- **Pinch of salt**
- **1 1/2 cups dry-roasted peanuts**
- **1 teaspoon pure vanilla extract**
- **1 teaspoon baking soda**
- **Vegetable oil, for spatula**

Brush a 9" x 13" baking sheet with butter; set aside. Combine sugar, corn syrup, cold water, and salt in a 3-quart saucepan. Bring to a boil over medium-high heat, stirring until sugar has dissolved. Using a pastry brush dipped in water, brush away any sugar crystals on the side of the pan to prevent re-crystallization. Cook, gently swirling occasionally, until mixture reaches 238F (soft-ball stage) on a candy thermometer. Stir in peanuts; continue to cook, stirring often so the nuts do not burn, until the mixture is golden amber in color, 284F (hard-crack stage) on thermometer. Remove from heat. Add butter, vanilla, and baking soda, gently stirring. The mixture will foam up in the pan. Lightly coat a metal spatula with oil. Pour the mixture on to the prepared baking sheet, and quickly spread, thinning into a 1/2-inch layer with the prepared spatula. Set the tray aside until completely cool. About 3 hours. Break brittle into pieces; store in an airtight container at room temperature up to 1 month. Makes about 1 pound.

Candied Grapefruit Peel

Candied fruit is a truly a traditional sweet, as sugar's main function for many years was to preserve fruits, nuts and, edible flowers. This recipe boils away the bitterness of a rind, adding a sweetness that joins the fruit flavor perfectly.

- 1 grapefruit
- 2 cups granulated sugar
- 1 1/4 cups water
- 1/2 cup superfine sugar for coating

Thoroughly wash and dry entire grapefruit. Using a sharp knife, cut off 1" from both top and bottom of grapefruit. Cut grapefruit in half from top to bottom. Use a large spoon to remove the inside flesh cleanly from peel. Cut the peel into 1/4" wide strips. Place strips of peel into medium saucepan and cover with cold water. Bring to a boil. Let strips continue to boil for one minute. Drain and repeat process three times. Put the sugar and water into the saucepan and gently bring to a boil. Drop in grapefruit strips. Poach gently for about 1 1/2 hours. Take grapefruit from the heat and allow the strips to cool in poaching water for 1/2 hour. Place strips on a rack to cool completely. Once grapefruit strips are at room temperature, roll them in fine sugar. Store at room temperature in airtight container for up to 4 weeks. Makes about 30 pieces.

Thirty-Minute Caramels

These delicious caramels are a quick and easy variation on traditional cream caramels. For extra taste and texture, add a cup of toasted, chopped walnuts before pouring out to cool.

- 1 cup unsalted butter
- 1 cup packed brown sugar
- 1 cup granulated sugar
- 1 1/4 cups sweetened condensed milk (1-14 oz. can)
- 1 1/2 cups light corn syrup
- 1/4 teaspoon salt
- 1/2 teaspoon pure vanilla extract

Butter a 9" square baking pan; set aside. In a heavy 4-quart saucepan, slowly melt the butter. Then add both brown and granulated sugars, condensed milk, corn syrup, and salt. Place over medium heat. Bring to a boil, stirring often with a wooden spoon. Reduce heat to the lowest setting that will maintain a boil. Using a candy thermometer, heat to 238F (soft-ball stage), stirring constantly to prevent scorching. Remove from heat, stir in vanilla. Immediately pour into pan but do not scrape excess from saucepan. Cool at room temperature until firm. Cut into 1" squares. Wrap each piece in clear cellophane or wax paper. Makes about 80 pieces, or 2 3/4 pounds. Store at room temperature in an airtight container for up to 3 weeks.

Chocolate Fudge

Some say that fudge was formed by mistake when a batch of caramels went awry. Tasting the foiled candy, the cook proclaimed, "Oh fudge." It seems to me that although fudge's cousin, caramel, wasn't formed, something went very right in the kitchen the day fudge was created.

- 6 tablespoons cocoa powder
- 4 cups granulated sugar
- 2/3 cup milk
- 4 tablespoons cold water
- 6 ounces semi-sweet chocolate, finely chopped
- 4 tablespoons unsalted butter
- 4 tablespoons light corn syrup
- 2 teaspoons pure vanilla extract
- 2 cup chopped walnuts

Butter an 8" x 8" baking pan; set aside. Prepare an ice bath in a large bowl. Sift cocoa and sugar into medium bowl. In a 3-quart saucepan, combine milk and cocoa powder mix. Mix with a wooden spoon until a sandy paste is formed. Add water, chocolate, butter, and corn syrup. Cook on medium heat, stirring constantly until sugar has completely dissolved, 7 to 10 minutes. If sugar crystals are present on side of pan, brush sides with a pastry brush. Allow mixture to come to a boil. Stop stirring and adjust the heat to the lowest setting that will maintain boil. Clip on candy thermometer and cook mixture to 236F (soft-ball stage). Remove from heat and hold pan on ice bath for one minute. Transfer pan to heat proof surface and let sit for 45 minutes or until thermometer registers 121F. Add vanilla extract and, using a wooden spoon, stir briskly until fudge loses its sheen, about 4 minutes. Stir in chopped walnuts. Quickly spread fudge mix into prepared pan with wooden spoon. Smooth fudge with lightly buttered knife until even. Score the top into 1" squares. Cover with plastic and let stand for 2 hours. Once cool and firm, cut into squares. Store in air-tight container at room temperature up to 2 weeks. Makes about 30 pieces.

Gum Drops

Treat yourself to a set of molds, extracts, and a collection of food colors, and you'll be able to create gummies in various shapes, flavors, and colors.

- 1 3/4 ounces powdered fruit pectin
- 3/4 cup water
- 1/2 teaspoon baking soda
- 1 cup granulated sugar
- 1 cup light corn syrup
- 2 teaspoons orange or strawberry extract
- 6-8 drops food coloring, orange or red
- Superfine sugar for coating
- Vegetable oil for coating molds

Combine fruit pectin, water, and baking soda in a 2-quart saucepan; mixture will foam. In a separate 3-quart pan, combine sugar and corn syrup. Place both saucepans over high heat. Cook, stirring alternately, until the foam disappears from the fruit pectin mixture and the sugar mixture boils rapidly, about 5 minutes. Turn off heat for pectin mix and cover pan with a lid. Clip candy thermometer to inside pan of sugar mix and continue to boil until mixture reaches 260F (hard-ball stage). Slowly pour heated fruit pectin mix into boiling sugar in a thin stream, until all pectin mix is added. Bring combined mixture to a boil, stirring constantly. Remove saucepan from heat and stir in extract, flavoring, and a few drops of coordinated food coloring. Immediately pour mixture into prepared candy molds. Allow to stand at room temperature (do not refrigerate) for about 4 hours, or until candy is cool and firm. Sprinkle the tops with superfine sugar. Remove from molds and roll entire shape in superfine sugar. Store in an airtight container at room temperature for up to 3 weeks. Makes one pound.

Green Gum Drops

extract = oil of anise; food coloring = green

Yellow Gum Drops

extract = oil of lemon; food coloring = yellow

Lollipops

These favorites are quick and fun to make hard candies. If you use molds, be sure to use those designed for high temperatures.

- Vegetable oil for greasing molds
- 1 cup granulated sugar
- 1/3 cup hot water
- 1/4 teaspoon cream of tartar
- 1/3 cup light com syrup
- 1/2 teaspoon liquid food color
- 1/2 teaspoon oil-based flavoring
- 12 lollipop sticks

Lightly brush ten small lollipop molds or other heatproof molds with vegetable oil or use a light coat of vegetable non-stick spray. Place molds on oiled cookie sheet. If not using molds, oil two large cookie sheets and line with parchment paper. Oil parchment paper and set sheets aside. Combine sugar, hot water, cream of tartar, and corn syrup in a heavy, 2-quart saucepan. Place on high heat and stir with a wooden spoon until all sugar crystals are dissolved. If sugar crystals are present, wash down sides of pan with a pastry brush dipped in hot water. Clip on thermometer. Continue cooking on high heat, without stirring, to 300F (hard-crack stage), then remove from heat. Entire cooking process takes about 10 minutes. Allow syrup to cool to 270F and add food color and flavoring and stir to blend. For suckers from molds, pour into prepared molds. Set the pan aside and place sticks centered into poured syrup. Cool candy molds at room temperature, about 20 minutes. Unmold and lay on a paper towel to absorb oil. When completely cool, wrap tightly in plastic wrap until ready to use. Store at room temperature up to 6 weeks.

For freeform "puddle" suckers, using half of syrup, slowly pour 2" circles on paper, leaving 4" between each. Set the pan with remaining syrup aside, and, moving rapidly, place sticks centered on poured syrup. Pour remaining syrup over circles. Let harden at room temperature, about 10 minutes. When completely cool, wrap tightly in plastic wrap until ready to use. Store at room temperature up to 6 weeks.

Marshmallows

Fresh-made marshmallows really take a cup of hot chocolate up a notch. Try some dipped in tempered chocolate or layer a soft marshmallow cube on a fresh made caramel.

- Butter to coat pan
- 2 envelopes (2 tablespoons) unflavored gelatin
- 1/2 cup cold water
- 1cup light corn syrup
- 2 cups granulated sugar
- 3/4 cup hot water (about 115°F)
- 1/4 teaspoon salt
- 1 teaspoon vanilla extract
- 1/2 cup confectioners sugar

Lightly butter bottom and sides of a 9" rectangular metal baking pan and dust bottom and sides with some confectioners sugar; set aside. In a large bowl sprinkle gelatin over cold water and let stand to soften, about 5 minutes. Pour 1/4 cup corn syrup over the softened gelatin. This mixture can sit while you proceed to next step. In a 2-quart heavy saucepan combine remaining corn syrup, granulated sugar, hot water, and salt over high heat. Stir with a wooden spoon, until mixture comes to a boil. If sugar crystals are present on side of pan, brush sides with a pastry brush. Clip on candy thermometer and cook on high heat, without stirring, until a candy thermometer registers 238°F (softball stage), about 12 minutes. Remove pan from heat and pour sugar mixture over gelatin mixture, stirring until gelatin is dissolved. With electric mixer, beat mixture on high speed until white thick, and lukewarm, about 10 minutes. Stir in vanilla. Pour mixture into baking pan and sift 1/4 cup confectioners sugar evenly over top. Allow marshmallow to sit, uncovered, until firm, at least 3 hours, and up to 1 day. Run a thin knife around edges of pan and invert pan onto a large cutting board. Lifting up one corner of inverted pan, with fingers loosen marshmallow and let drop onto cutting board. With a large knife trim edges of marshmallow and cut marshmallow into roughly 1" cubes. Sift remaining confectioners sugar into a large bowl and add marshmallows in batches, tossing to evenly coat. Marshmallows keep in an airtight container at cool room temperature for 1 week. Makes about 30 pieces.

Non Pareils

Nonpareils are dark chocolate dollops topped with sugar beads. The name for these simple French candies means "without peer," meaning they are unmatched. The white drops resting on the chocolate peaks resemble snow covered mountains.

- 8 oz. bittersweet chocolate
- 1/2 teaspoon pure vegetable shortening
- 1/4 cup white sugar beads

Line a baking sheet with parchment paper. In the top of a double boiler or in a heat-proof bowl set over a pan of simmering water. Melt the chocolate and shortening, stirring with a rubber spatula until smooth. Spoon the melted chocolate into 1/2" circles onto prepared baking sheet. Cool for 15 minutes, then sprinkle with sugar beads. Let non pareils harden in a cool place for 4 hours before serving. Makes about 50 candies. Store non pareils in an airtight container at a cool temperature for six weeks.

Nougat

Nougat is much loved in southern Europe. It is light and nutty — a really delicious confection.

- 1/2 cup confectioners sugar, for dusting
- 9 fluid oz. honey
- 1 1/3 cups granulated sugar
- 1/4 cup water
- 2 large egg whites
- Pinch of salt
- 4 cups slivered almonds, lightly toasted, chopped
- 1 cup shelled, unsalted pistachios, chopped

Line a 12" x 18" baking sheet with parchment paper and sprinkle generously with confectioners sugar. Set aside. Combine honey, sugar and water in heavy medium saucepan. Stir over medium heat until sugar dissolves. Increase heat to high and boil, without stirring. Attach candy thermometer and boil syrup to 238F (soft-ball stage). Meanwhile, using electric mixer, beat egg whites with pinch of salt in medium bowl until soft peaks form. Continue to cook mixture to 284F (soft-crack stage). Remove from heat, with mixer running. Gradually pour hot syrup over egg white mixture, beating constantly. Continue beating on high speed until very stiff and lukewarm, about 4 minutes. Remove bowl from mixer and stir in nuts. Spread nougat into the prepared pan. Pat or roll into 3/4" thickness. Sprinkle more confectioners sugar on top. Let set for 3 hours or until firm. Cut with sharp knife into squares or diamonds. Store in airtight container up to 3 weeks.

Cherry Taffy

This taffy can be flavored with any fruit jam or marmalade. Substitute your favorite flavor for the suggested cherry. Instead of pulling, which makes taffy porous and airy, this taffy slab is cooled in a pan, which results in a taffy hunk that reminds me of Tangy Taffy or Doscher's French Chew.

- 1/4 teaspoon unsalted butter for greasing pan
- 1 large egg white
- 2 1/2 cups granulated sugar
- 1/2 cup water
- 1/4 teaspoon cream of tartar
- 1 cup of cherry preserves
- 5 drops red food coloring

Butter an 11" x 17" pan with high edges. Line the pan with wax paper and butter the paper; set aside. In a large bowl, beat the egg white until a soft peak forms; set aside. Combine the sugar, water, and cream of tartar in a heavy 3-quart pan. Over medium heat, stir mixture with a wooden spoon until it comes to a boil. Clip on candy thermometer to inside of the pan and continue to cook without stirring until the mixture reaches 260F (hard-ball stage). If sugar crystals are present on side of pan, brush sides with a pastry brush. Add preserves and food coloring. Stir with wooden spoon until preserves mix completely into syrup. Bring back to a boil until thermometer registers 260F again. Turn off heat. Revive egg white with a quick beating before slowly adding hot syrup. Continue mixing until mixture is warm and stiff, about 10 minutes. Lightly coat a metal spatula with oil. Pour the mixture into the prepared baking pan and quickly spread, thinning into a 1/2" layer with the prepared spatula. Set the tray aside until completely cool, about 3 hours. Once cool, cut taffy with buttered scissors. Wrap pieces in wax paper and store in airtight container at room temperature for up to 2 weeks.

Buttercream Truffles

Originally named for their similarity in shape to the highly prized mushrooms, chocolate truffles are deliciously decadent. Truffle density allows flavors to really come through. This recipe is an easy version made with a butter and cream center. Substitute other liquors for rum to enhance the chocolate flavor.

- 6 ounces of unsweetened chocolate
- 2/3 cup softened unsalted butter
- 2 1/3 cups confectioners sugar
- 1/3 cup heavy cream
- 1 tablespoon rum
- Sweetened cocoa powder for coating

In the top of a double boiler or in a pan of simmering water, set in a heatproof bowl. Completely melt the chocolate, stirring with a rubber spatula until smooth. Set melted chocolate aside. Combine the softened butter and confectioners sugar in a large mixing bowl. Mix on medium speed until mixture turns into a smooth pale yellow paste. Turn the mixer to low speed and beat in heavy cream. Add the melted chocolate and rum until mix becomes a smooth paste. Tightly cover and refrigerate chocolate buttercream for several hours until it is cool and firm. Scoop out teaspoon of chocolate buttercream, and, with hands, roll into a ball. If chocolate becomes too warm, place back in refrigerator. Roll rounded truffles in sweetened cocoa powder and store in an airtight container for up to 2 weeks. Truffles should be served at room temperature.

ACKNOWLEDGEMENTS

This book was made possible by the many people who helped me, guided me, and shared candy with me. Countless companies and individuals gave their time, opened their archives, and recounted personal experiences.

Ted Shepherd, Susan Ryba, and Myrna Fossum, along with many other Fannie May folks, were influential to my candy career. While Christine Keller, Dan Driscoll, and Sara Runde made candy extra fun and always kept it interesting.

Michael Edwards graciously and promptly built the tight, very well-received proposal design. Eric Rayman kindly lent me his industry expertise. He guided me through details and was open and supportive, even while working on his own publishing project. Joanne Camas was an early adopter editor whom I met via Conde Nast. Lisa Ashcraft gave me the confidence to believe that things are very possible even without agents.

Kate Cunningham accompanied me to factories, while Tamara Staples shot the interiors. Tamara's incredible portfolio can be viewed at www.tamarastaples.com. In addition to being patient readers and great behind the camera, both are supportive and lovely friends.

This book was ultimately compiled by the companies profiled that helped me gather and verify the necessary information. Tomi Holt, publicist for Jelly Belly, went above and beyond, supplying historical and industry details. She's fiercely knowledgeable about her business. The National Confectioners Association helped me to reach out to the very busy, and sometimes not so talkative, confection industry. They thankfully backed the book early on.

Several writers inspired and versed me. Tim Richardson's book appeared as I was completing mine and was a great and welcome read. Ray Broekel's books have been a favorite resource since my Chicago candy days. I relate to his Evanston upbringing and love for candy. Jöel Glenn Brenner wrote a fascinating book on chocolate; it should some day become a movie.

I magically bonded with the candy collectors out there. Michael Rosenberg has a candy company along with an amazing collection of ephemera, displays, wrappers, and other candy material. His vast collection helped make the book come alive with visual excitement. Visiting his private museum provided a great research opportunity and confirmed the validity of the concept. Jeff Nelson of Dischord Records has an extensive, well-preserved gum collection. Jeff hosted me and photographer Tamara Staples for an awesome night of gum viewing and chewing. Dan Goodsell has gathered great old-school food, toy, and candy items. They can be found at www.theimaginaryworld.com. He contributed some iconic, graphic-rich packaging from his righteous collection.

My business partner, Will Noonan, tolerated much candy nonsense. He is a complete candy snob but was fully supportive of this creation. Ann was a wise reader, sweetening her valid comments with great stories. Meaghan served as an important advisor all along the way, and later she and Con gave me a deluxe respite where I could get down to business. Lastly, my sister Kate, with whom I have shared much yummy candy and delicious moments, is simply and consistently there.

Thanks to the following companies for the use of their candy for this book cover: Hershey, Tootsie Roll, Spangler, Goetze, Jelly Belly, and Kencraft. Special thanks to Collectors Press. They helped make this book possible, readable, and exciting to look at.

CREDITS

All photos and images are copyrighted © by the companies and artists that produced and own them.
Products may have been mentioned without their ® registered trademark.
Michael Rosenberg, Promotion in Motion Archives
Dan Goodsell Collection, www.theimaginaryworld.com
Tamara Staples Photography, www.tamarastaples.com

BIBLIOGRAPHY

Near A Thousand Tables, by Felipe Fernandez-Armesto, The Free Press, 2002
Sweets: A History of Candy, by Tim Richardson, Bloomsbury, 2002
The Ultimate Candy Book, by Bruce Weinstein, Harper Collins, 2000
The Emperors Of Chocolate, by Jöel Glenn Brenner, Random House, 1999
The Food Chronology, by James Trager, Henry Holt and Company, 1995
History of Food, by Maguelonne Toussaint-Samat, Blackwell, 1992
The Chocolate Chronicles, by Ray Broekel, Wallace Homestead, 1985
The Great American Candy Bar Book, by Ray Broekel, Houghton Mifflin Company, 1982
Food in History, by Reay Tannahil, Stein and Day, 1973
The Fannie Farmer Cookbook, Dexter and Wilma Lord Perkins, Little Brown and Company, 1965

PLACES TO PURCHASE CLASSIC CANDY

Dylan's Candy Bar is the brainchild of co-founders and owners Dylan Lauren and Jeff Rubin. Their amazing stores offer more than 5,000 different choices of sweets, including a vast assortment of American classics.

1011 Third Ave., New York City

(646) 735-0078

www.dylanscandybar.com

McKeesport Candy Co., established in 1927, is one of the oldest independently owned candy wholesalers in the nation.

(888) 525-7577

www.CandyFavorites.com

CANDY MAKING SUPPLIES AND CLASSES

The Institute of Culinary Education, formerly Peter Kump's, is one of the oldest and most prestigious culinary schools in the United States and a New York institution.

50 West 23rd Street, New York City

(212) 847-0700

www.iceculinary.com

New York Cake and Baking

56 West 22nd Street, New York City

(212) 675-2253